# TRAILBLAZERS
## IN SCIENCE AND TECHNOLOGY

# Rosalind Franklin

## PHOTOGRAPHING BIOMOLECULES

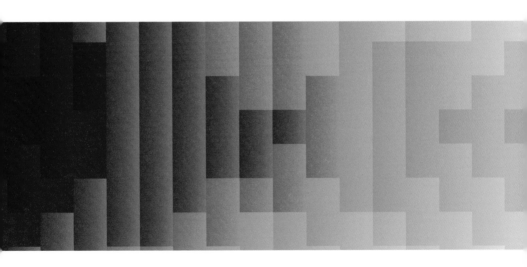

# TRAILBLAZERS
## IN SCIENCE AND TECHNOLOGY

# Rosalind Franklin

## PHOTOGRAPHING BIOMOLECULES

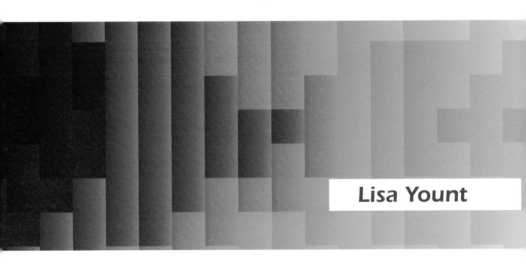

Lisa Yount

CHELSEA HOUSE
An Infobase Learning Company

**ROSALIND FRANKLIN: Photographing Biomolecules**

Copyright © 2012 by Lisa Yount

Chelsea House
An imprint of Infobase Learning
132 West 31st Street
New York NY 10001

**Library of Congress Cataloging-in-Publication Data**

Yount, Lisa.
  Rosalind Franklin : photographing biomolecules / Lisa Yount.
    p. cm. — (Trailblazers in science and technology)
  Includes bibliographical references and index.
  ISBN 978-1-60413-660-9
  1. Franklin, Rosalind, 1920–1958—Juvenile literature. 2. Molecular biologists—Great Britain—Biography—Juvenile literature. 3. Women molecular biologists—Great Britain—Biography—Juvenile literature. 4. DNA—History—Juvenile literature. I. Title.
  QH506.Y68 2011
  572.8092—dc22
  [B]                                              2010048229

Chelsea House books are available at special discounts when purchased in bulk quantities for businesses, associations, institutions, or sales promotions. Please call our Special Sales Department in New York at (212) 967-8800 or (800) 322-8755.

You can find Chelsea House on the World Wide Web at http://www.infobaselearning.com

Text design by Erika K. Arroyo
Composition by Hermitage Publishing Services
Illustrations by Bobbi McCutcheon
Photo research by Suzanne M. Tibor
Cover printed by Bang Printing, Brainerd, Minn.
Book printed and bound by Bang Printing, Brainerd, Minn.
Date printed: October 2011
Printed in the United States of America

10 9 8 7 6 5 4 3 2 1

This book is printed on acid-free paper.

To Verah, for being such a good friend

# Contents

# Preface

Trailblazers in Science and Technology is a multivolume set of biographies for young adults that profiles 10 individuals or small groups who were trailblazers in science—in other words, those who made discoveries that greatly broadened human knowledge and sometimes changed society or saved many lives. In addition to describing those discoveries and their effects, the books explore the qualities that made these people trailblazers, the personal relationships they formed, and the way those relationships interacted with their scientific work.

What does it take to be a trailblazer, in science or any other field of human endeavor?

First, a trailblazer must have imagination: the power to envision a path where others see only expanses of jungle, desert, or swamp. Helen Taussig, Alfred Blalock, and Vivien Thomas imagined an operation that could help children whose condition everyone else thought was hopeless. Louis and Mary Leakey looked at shards of bone embedded in the rocks of an African valley and pictured in them the story of humanity's birth.

Imagination alone will not blaze a trail, however. A trailblazer must also have determination and courage, the will to keep on trudging and swinging a metaphorical machete long after others fall by the wayside. Pierre and Marie Curie stirred their witch's cauldron for day after day in a dirty shed, melting down tons of rock to extract a tiny sample of a strange new element. The women astronomers who assisted Edward Pickering patiently counted and compared white spots on thousands of photographs in order to map the universe.

Because their vision is so different from that of others, trailblazers often are not popular. They may find themselves isolated even from those who are working toward the same goals, as Rosalind Franklin did in her research on DNA. Other researchers may brand them as outsiders and therefore ignore their work, as mathematicians did at first with Edward Lorenz's writings on chaos theory because Lorenz's background was in meteorology (weather science), a quite different scientific discipline. Society may regard them as eccentric or worse, as happened to electricity pioneer Nikola Tesla and, to a lesser extent, genome analyst and entrepreneur Craig Venter. This separateness sometimes freed and sometimes hindered these individuals' creative paths.

On the other hand, the relationships that trailblazers do form often sustain them and enrich their work. In addition to supplying emotional and intellectual support, compatible partners of whatever type can build on one another's ideas to achieve insights that neither would have been likely to develop alone. Two married couples described in this set, the Curies and the Leakeys, not only helped each other in their scientific efforts but inspired some of their children to continue on their path. Other partnerships, such as the one between Larry Page and Sergey Brin, the computer scientists-turned-entrepreneurs who founded the Internet giant Google, related strictly to business, but they were just as essential to the partners' success.

Even relationships that have an unhealthy side may prove to offer unexpected benefits. Pickering hired women such as Williamina Fleming to be his astronomical "computers" because he could pay them far less than he would have had to give men for the same work. Similarly, Alfred Blalock took advantage of Vivien Thomas's limited work choices as an African American to keep Thomas at his command in the surgical laboratory. At the same time, these instances of exploitation, so typical of the society of the times, gave the "exploited" opportunities that they would not otherwise have had. Thomas would not have contributed to lifesaving surgeries if he had remained a carpenter in Nashville, even though he might have earned more money than he did by working for Blalock. Fleming surely would never have discovered her talent for astronomy if Pickering had kept her as merely his "Scottish maid."

Competitors can form almost as close a relationship as cooperative partners, and like the irritating grain of sand in an oyster's shell that eventually yields a pearl, rivalries can inspire scientific trailblazers to heights of achievement that they might not have attained if they had worked unopposed. Tesla's competition with Thomas Edison to establish a grid of electrical power around U.S. cities stimulated as well as infuriated both men. Venter's announcement that he would produce a readout of humanity's genes sooner than the massive, government-funded Human Genome Project (HGP) pushed him, as well as his rival, HGP leader Francis Collins, to greater efforts. The French virologist Luc Montagnier was spurred to refine and prove his suspicions about the virus he thought was linked to AIDS because he knew that Robert Gallo, a similar researcher in another country, was close to publishing the same conclusions.

It is our hope that the biographies in the Trailblazers in Science and Technology set will inspire young people not only to discover and nurture the trailblazer within themselves but also to trust their imagination, even when it shows them a path that others say cannot exist, yet at the same time hold it to strict standards of proof. We hope they will form supportive relationships with others who share their vision, yet will also be willing to learn from those they compete with or even dislike. Above all, we hope they will feel the curiosity about the natural world and the determination to unravel its secrets that all trailblazers of science share.

# Acknowledgments

I would like to thank Frank K. Darmstadt for his help and suggestions, Suzie Tibor for rounding up the photographs, Bobbi McCutcheon for doing the line drawings, my cats for keeping me company (helpfully or otherwise), and, as always, my husband, Harry Henderson, for—well—everything.

# Introduction

In order to understand how something works, one must know how it is built. Humans can speak, walk, and carry objects because of the way their bodies are constructed. The same is true of molecules, the combinations of atoms that form the units of chemical compounds. A molecule's structure determines, for instance, what other kinds of atoms and molecules can attach to it by means of chemical or electrical bonds. Structure has even greater effect on the function of the large, complex molecules that make up the bodies of living things.

By the middle of the 20th century, scientists were beginning to recognize this relationship between molecules' structure and functions. They could make little use of it, however, because determining the structure of complex molecules was almost impossible. Even the largest molecules were far too small to see with any kind of microscope available at the time. Chemists knew the numbers of different kinds of atoms in the molecules, and they sometimes could identify smaller molecules that combine to form larger ones, but they could not tell how these atoms or smaller molecules were arranged.

The technique of *X-ray crystallography,* invented in 1912, had been used to work out the structure of simple molecules that combine in regular patterns called *crystals.* Scientists photographed the crystals with cameras that use X-rays instead of light, producing pictures that consist of dark dots or streaks on a light background. Measuring these marks and applying mathematical calculations to them provided a glimpse of the molecules' shape. A few researchers in the 1930s and 1940s began to apply this technique to complex molecules that did not form obvious crystals, but the results were much less clear than with simple substances. Interpreting the resulting photographs remained more of an art than a science.

# REASONS FOR FAME

Rosalind Franklin (1920–58), a British scientist, became an expert in the scientific art of using X-ray crystallography to reveal the structure of complex biomolecules (molecules found in living things). In her all-too-brief career, cut short by cancer, she interpreted three very different types of substances. She first investigated coal and other forms of carbon, the remains of plants and animals that lived in the prehistoric past. She then turned her attention to DNA *(deoxyribonucleic acid),* the compound that scientists were just beginning to recognize as the carrier of inherited, or genetic, information. Finally, she helped to work out the structure of *viruses,* complex molecules that can reproduce and cause disease in living organisms.

Valuable as they are, these contributions in themselves are only one of the reasons why Rosalind Franklin deserves to be remembered. Although Franklin's studies of DNA represent only a small part of her scientific work, they played a key role in what Aaron Klug (1926–  ), Franklin's collaborator in the later part of her career, called (in an article on the discovery of DNA in Torsten Krude's *DNA: Changing Science and Society)* "one of the greatest discoveries in biology in the twentieth century": the discovery of the structure of the DNA molecule, which showed how that molecule could encode genetic information and reproduce itself. James Watson (1928–  ) and Francis Crick (1916–2004), the two men who worked out DNA's structure, gained clues from Franklin's work so valuable that they might not have been able to find the structure without them.

Franklin has also become famous because her part in the DNA discovery and her relationship to several of the other scientists involved in it bring up serious issues of scientific ethics. One is the question of credit. Scientists normally build on the work of their predecessors and contemporaries, but they are expected to name those other researchers in their published papers. They are also expected to ask permission to use any experimental data from others that has not yet appeared in print. Critics have maintained that Watson and Crick violated both of these rules: They used some of Franklin's data without her knowledge, and they never fully gave credit to her in their writings.

Franklin's role in the discovery of DNA raises the issue of discrimination against women in science as well. Feminist writers such as Anne Sayre, a friend of Franklin's and author of the biography *Rosalind Franklin and DNA,* have claimed that Watson, Crick, and Maurice Wilkins (1916–2004), the assistant director of the laboratory in which Franklin carried out her

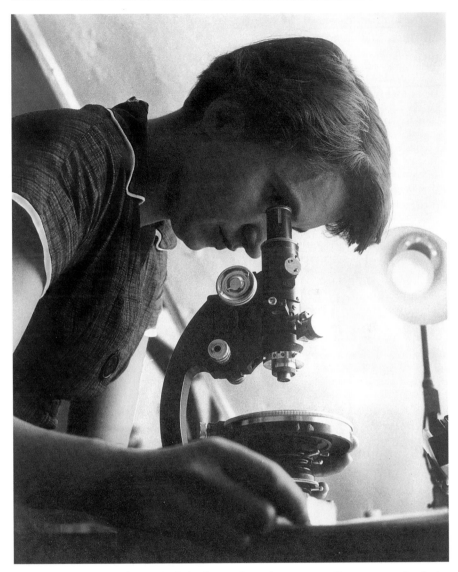

Rosalind Franklin, a British scientist, helped to work out the structure of important molecules in living things in the mid-20th century. Although she is shown here using a microscope, she did most of her work with photographs taken by cameras that used X-rays instead of light. (*Science Source/Photo Researchers, Inc.*)

DNA studies, felt free to "borrow" Franklin's research findings because she was a woman and therefore was regarded as less important than a male scientist in her position would have been. Sayre also felt that the personality conflict that arose between Franklin and Wilkins contained elements of discrimination. However, some other commentators, such as science historian Horace Freeland Judson, who wrote a history of the early work on DNA called *The Eighth Day of Creation,* believe that discrimination against women scientists did not play a major part in the difficulties Franklin experienced. The question of how much effect discrimination had on Rosalind Franklin's career remains controversial today.

## A VARIED CAREER

This volume in the Trailblazers of Science and Technology set describes Rosalind Franklin's life and career, the impact of her work on her chosen field of *physical chemistry* (which studies the effects of physics on chemistry) and beyond, the complex relationships between Franklin and other scientists, and the ethical issues raised by events in her career. Chapters 1 and 2 deal with her early life: Chapter 1 portrays her childhood and youth, ending with her education at Cambridge University, and chapter 2 covers her research on the structure of different forms of carbon, first as a member of the Coal Utilisation Research Association (CURA) in Britain during World War II and then as a researcher in a French chemistry laboratory in the late 1940s.

Chapters 3, 4, and 5 focus on Franklin's work on the structure of DNA at King's College, part of the University of London. Franklin saw her two years at King's as a relatively brief and unimportant, as well as unpleasant, interlude in her life. This period is worth examining in detail, however, because most of the fame she achieved after her death rests on it. Chapter 3 covers the first nine months of 1951, during which Franklin established herself in the laboratory nicknamed "Randall's Circus." Chapter 4 highlights Franklin's discoveries about DNA, as well as some misinterpretations that for a while led her to mistaken conclusions about the molecule. Chapter 5 describes her final months at King's, which were marked by a frantic "race" to solve the puzzle of DNA's structure. Franklin never saw herself as part of this race, yet her work played a crucial role in determining the competition's winners.

Chapter 6 describes the research that Franklin herself probably would have considered most important, her work on the structure of *tobacco mosaic virus.* Her discoveries about this virus, which causes a disease in tobacco plants, revealed important facts about the structure of other viruses as well, including some that produce illness in humans. Franklin's virus research, done at Birkbeck College (another college at the University of London), marked a return to happier days, in which she established her own research team and received some of the recognition that her merit as a scientist deserved. Unfortunately, they were cut short by ovarian cancer, which killed her in 1958 at the age of 37.

Some of the most important implications of Rosalind Franklin's research and much of the fame that has come to her appeared only after her death. These developments are recounted in chapter 7. They include the expansion of knowledge about DNA that Franklin's work at King's College had helped to begin, a caricature of Franklin in a rival scientist's best-selling book, and a rush by friends and supporters to defend and preserve her reputation. The chapter ends with a list of posthumous honors that have been given to Franklin in recent years. Finally, this book's conclusion shows ways in which the three fields to which Franklin contributed have continued to grow, providing a living legacy from this woman who, according to a memorial article about her by crystallography pioneer John Desmond Bernal (1901–71), made "among the most beautiful X-ray photographs . . . ever taken."

# Choosing Science

Rosalind Franklin's mother wrote of her in a privately printed biographical sketch, "All her life Rosalind knew exactly where she was going." Franklin knew by the time she was a teenager that she was going toward a career in science. She also knew that reaching that goal would not be easy. She had grown up with many advantages, but one handicap threatened to outweigh them all: She was a woman.

## ADVANTAGES AND COMPETITION

Rosalind Elsie Franklin's advantages began with her family. Her father, Ellis Franklin, was a banker in the firm of A. Keyser & Co., a private merchant bank. He owned a four-story house in the upscale Bayswater district of west London, and his five children, of whom Rosalind was the second, lacked for nothing. Born on July 25, 1920, Rosalind had an older brother, David; two younger ones, Colin and Roland; and finally, in 1929, a sister, Jenifer.

Both Ellis Franklin and his wife, the former Muriel Waley, belonged to Jewish families that had been prominent in British public life for hundreds of years. (Their ancestors had Anglicized their original family names, Fraenkel and Levi, soon after arriving in England in the 1700s.) Rosalind's great-uncle, Sir Herbert Samuel (later Viscount Samuel [1870–1963]), had been the first High Commissioner of the British Mandate for Palestine, a legal commission for the administration of Palestine. The Franklins had generally

Rosalind Franklin learned to hold her own in a houseful of brothers. She is shown here with her brothers and sister around 1932. *(Churchill Archives Centre, Churchill College, Cambridge)*

earned their livings in banking, trade, and publishing, the Waleys in academics and law.

In *Rosalind Franklin: The Dark Lady of DNA,* biographer Brenda Maddox wrote that Ellis Franklin "was a natural patriarch. Large, intelligent, amusing, successful, overbearing, he knew what was best for those around him and told them so." His wife, Muriel, spent much of her time working for various charities, a type of activity that both men and women in the Franklin family traditionally pursued. (Some Franklins were active in social and political causes as well, including socialism and women's rights.)

Like many other families of the time, the Franklins seldom showed affection in physical displays such as hugs and kisses. Nonetheless, they were close. Even when the children were nearly grown, they and their parents took vacations together, for instance. These were often vigorous outings, involving long hikes through the countryside or climbing mountains. Rosalind remained fond of these activities and close to her family all her life.

Competition was as much a part of Rosalind's home life as companionship. Growing up in a houseful of brothers ruled by a stern and opinionated father, Rosalind had to—and did—develop the strength to hold her own while surrounded by males. Both her skill in debate and her powerful intelligence showed themselves early. Rosalind's aunt, Helen ("Mamie") Bent-

Rosalind Franklin learned to love vigorous outdoor activities during shared vacations with her family, and she kept this interest all her life. She is seen here on a mountain-climbing trip in Norway in the 1940s. (*Churchill Archives Centre, Churchill College, Cambridge*)

wich, wrote of Rosalind when the girl was only six years old, "Rosalind is alarmingly clever—she spends all her time doing arithmetic for pleasure, and invariably gets her sums right."

Although Ellis and Muriel Franklin did their best to treat all their children equally, Rosalind sometimes felt that they favored her brothers, and she resented it. When she was nine years old, for instance, her parents sent her away to a boarding school on the British coast. According to Anne Sayre's *Rosalind Franklin and DNA,* they probably did so because a childhood illness had left Rosalind's health temporarily fragile, and they hoped that the sea air would make her stronger. She was terribly homesick at the school, however, and complained that none of her brothers had to leave home. She was allowed to return to London after two years.

## PREPARING FOR A CAREER

Rosalind's experiences were much happier at the St. Paul's School for Girls, the West London day school she attended from age 11. Founded in 1904, the school was an offshoot of the venerable St. Paul's School for Boys. Despite their names, the schools were not connected with any religion, and Jewish as well as Christian students attended them.

Rosalind's aunt and several cousins had been "Paulinas," as the students called themselves, so it was no surprise that Rosalind was sent there. This choice of school, however, also showed that Ellis and Muriel Franklin took their daughter's education seriously. St. Paul's was no mere finishing school, which was intended to teach wealthy young women how to behave in society; it had classes in mathematics, physics, biology, and chemistry. The first high mistress (head) of the school had written, "At St. Paul's . . . every girl is being prepared for a career. The High Mistress considers that no woman has a right to exist who does not live a useful life." At the time Rosalind Franklin entered the school, former Paulinas held important jobs in public life, civil service, medicine, publishing, and the law.

Rosalind thrived at St. Paul's. She excelled not only in the mathematics, physics, and chemistry classes—her favorites—but also in sports, including hockey and tennis. She also joined the school debating society. She did well enough to earn scholarships for her entire time there, although her family neither needed nor accepted the money. Additionally, she made lifelong friendships among the other students.

At home, meanwhile, Rosalind learned to share her parents' love of education and philanthropy. She heard a great deal about Ellis Franklin's favorite charity, the Working Men's School, which had been formed in 1854 to provide workers with an education that most could not otherwise afford. The school accomplished a second purpose, bringing people of different social classes together, by having volunteers teach its courses. Ellis Franklin, who had dreamed of becoming a scientist before family pressure pushed him into banking, spent several nights there each week giving classes in electricity, magnetism, and the history of World War I. The school's only drawback, in Rosalind's eyes, was that it took its name too literally: It admitted no women as either teachers or students.

## COLLEGE AND WAR

During Rosalind's last years as a Paulina, the threat of a new world war hung over Britain. Germany, headed by National Socialist (Nazi) leader Adolf Hitler (1869–1945), began conquering its European neighbors one after another in the late 1930s. Hitler and his government were fiercely anti-Semitic, and Jews—at least those lucky enough to have ways to do so—left Germany and its conquered territories, first in a trickle and then in droves. A number of these refugees came

Newnham College, shown here in 2008, is one of the two women's colleges that existed at Cambridge University in Rosalind Franklin's time. Franklin attended Newnham from 1938 to 1941. *(Mark Pink/Alamy)*

to Britain, where well-off Jews, including Franklin's parents, tried to find homes and jobs for them. Working with the German/Jewish Refugee Committee, Ellis Franklin helped some of the new arrivals obtain entry permits. Rosalind did her part by sorting papers during weekends and school holidays.

The Franklins also worked to find homes for orphaned and homeless Jewish children, first from Germany and then from Austria, which Germany took over in March 1938. The family even brought two of the Austrian children home to live with them. One was a nine-year-old girl, Evi Eisenstadter, who arrived in the summer of 1938; her father had been taken to Buchenwald, the infamous German concentration camp.

Rosalind, meanwhile, prepared for a university education. Her father thought her desire for advanced schooling unwise at first because he believed, as many people did at the time, that higher education simply made a woman unhappy and kept her from finding a marriage partner. He recommended that Rosalind spend her energy on volunteer work instead, as her mother and many other Franklin women had done. When his arguments failed to sway her, however, he did not try to stand in her way.

Rosalind applied to and was accepted at both Newnham and Girton, the two women's colleges of Britain's prestigious Cambridge University, but she ultimately chose Newnham. She won a "leaving scholarship" of 30 pounds from St. Paul's because she placed first in the Cambridge entrance examinations in chemistry. Her father insisted on giving the money to a student who

## WOMEN AT CAMBRIDGE UNIVERSITY: LONG ROAD TO ACCEPTANCE

Women who wished to obtain an education, particularly in science, have faced an uphill struggle throughout most of Western history, but the struggle was particularly hard at Cambridge University. Cambridge, one of England's two premier universities (the other is Oxford), has existed since the 13th century, but women did not enter its doors until 1870—and they remained second-class citizens until 1947, two years after Rosalind Franklin earned her Ph.D.

In Britain, each university is composed of a number of colleges. Both of the colleges for women that existed in Franklin's time had been founded in the 1870s. Women were first allowed to attend lectures at Cambridge in 1870, and Newnham, the college Franklin attended, began in 1871 as a boardinghouse for women who wanted to go to the lectures regularly but did not live nearby. It became a college of Cambridge in 1875. Girton, the other women's college, started as a separate college for women in 1869 and became a Cambridge college in 1873.

Women gained the right to take the university's Tripos examinations (the final examinations for a bachelor's degree, given in several parts during the years of undergraduate training) in 1881, and they were granted certificates if they passed. The university awarded degrees to women after 1921, but for several decades these were merely "degrees titular." The titular degrees represented the same academic achievement as degrees received by men, but they did not allow women to take part in university government, as male graduates could. Women were made full members of the university and granted degrees completely equivalent to those of men in 1947.

The status of women at the University of London, in two of whose colleges (King's College and Birkbeck College) Franklin later worked, was very different. Women attended lectures at Birkbeck as early as 1830, and the university opened its examinations, the gateway to degrees, to women in 1878. The University of London awarded its first degrees to women—the first university degrees for women in the country—in 1882, 65 years before lagging Cambridge followed suit.

would benefit from financial aid, but he was very proud of the honor that the scholarship represented.

## STUDIES UNDER FIRE

Germany's chancellor Adolf Hitler and British prime minister Neville Chamberlain (1869–1940) signed a nonaggression pact called the Munich Agreement in September 1938, but some Britons believed that the "peace in our time" that Chamberlain promised was merely a dangerous illusion. They suspected that Hitler would attack England as soon as the German leader felt strong enough. At most, Chamberlain might have bought the country a little time to prepare its defense. By the time Rosalind Franklin went to Cambridge in October, some Londoners were beginning to build bomb shelters. However, in that quiet college town 50 miles (80 km) north of the capital, few spoke of a possible war.

Franklin took classes in mathematics, mineralogy, physics, and chemistry during her first year. Although she was not especially interested in biology, some of her courses introduced her to the complex molecules that make up living things. She learned about *proteins,* the workhorse chemicals of the cell, and *nucleic acids,* that are part of *chromosomes,* the bodies in cells that carry inherited information. She heard about viruses, mysterious particles that could cause disease but could also form crystals much like those made by simple inorganic compounds such as table salt. She also continued her enjoyment of sports, including hockey and tennis. She took little part in the social life of the college, however, preferring to spend time with her relatives and old friends from her St. Paul's days.

Britain declared war on Germany on September 3, 1939, after Nazi troops invaded Poland, and some English citizens expected a rain of German bombs to follow soon. They set up air raid shelters in London Underground (subway) stations and staged drills to teach people how to reach safe locations quickly when alarms sounded. Homes and businesses put up blackout curtains to block light that might guide marauding planes, and families learned to use their ugly but protective gas masks.

Students at Cambridge had their drills too, since the town was located near several Royal Air Force bases and therefore might become a target for German bombs. When sirens announced an air raid alert, everyone was supposed to leave the university buildings and go down to protective trenches that had been dug. Franklin was assigned to wake 10 people during any alert that occurred at night. She found the drills annoying because they interrupted her studies, and she hated spending time in the trenches because she suffered from mild claustrophobia (fear of enclosed spaces). In those early days of the war, before German attacks on Britain had begun, Franklin was far from alone in feeling that the risk of such attacks had been exaggerated.

Franklin's future educational path would depend on her performance on a set of examinations called the Tripos, possibly named after the three-legged stool on which students had once been forced to sit while taking the exams. She took the first part of her Tripos in May 1940, just as German armies were poised to take over France and Winston Churchill (1874–1965) succeeded Neville Chamberlain as Britain's prime minister. She feared that she had done badly, but in fact she took a top place, high enough to win a scholarship for her final year as an undergraduate.

Franklin and the other members of her class were not sure they would still have a university in which to study when their senior year came. The long-expected bombing of Britain began in July 1940, raining devastation on London and other large cities. No planes attacked Cambridge, but the war was taking away so many students and faculty members that everyone feared the university might have to close. Some left to serve in the military or do civilian war work, while others with apparent ties to Germany—even Jewish refugees who had fled that country—were forced into internment camps. "Practically the whole of the Cavendish have disappeared," Franklin wrote to her parents in October 1940, speaking of the staff of Cambridge's famed physics laboratory. "Biochemistry was almost entirely run by Germans and may not survive." Nonetheless, Franklin was pleased that the school's disturbed routine gave her more opportunity for independent work than she would have had in more normal times. She could stay in the laboratory all day if she wanted to, and she frequently did.

German bombing reached a new intensity during the Blitz (from a German word meaning "lightning"), which began on September 7, 1940. At the start of this campaign, which lasted until May 1941, German planes bombed London every night for 57 days. Attacks on British cities during the Blitz killed thousands of people and destroyed millions of homes and other buildings. Franklin was bound to have worried about her family, who were still living in London. The senior Franklins were spared, but after a raid in November blew out their windows and killed two women in a house nearby, they followed the example of many other Londoners by moving to the countryside for the duration of the war. When Germany added incendiary (fire) bombs to the attacks in early 1941, Franklin volunteered as a fire watcher, whose job was to put out the devices as they landed.

# DEGREE TITULAR

During Franklin's last year at Cambridge, the university replaced some of its lost staff with European scholars who fled to England after the German juggernaut swallowed their home countries. One of these, a French-Jewish physicist named Adrienne Weill, arrived in fall 1940. Weill, who had studied under the renowned Marie Curie (1867–1934), began doing research at the Cavendish and was also, as Franklin put it in one of her letters home, "adopted" by Newnham.

Franklin heard Weill lecture on Curie and, Brenda Maddox writes, was "deeply impressed by this elegant cosmopolitan woman of science and public affairs." When the two were introduced, Franklin learned, furthermore, that Weill's mother, a well-known leader in the early crusade for women's rights, was a good friend of Franklin's famous great-uncle, Viscount Samuel. Franklin wrote her parents that Weill was "a delightful person, full of good stories and most interesting to talk to on any scientific or political subject." Franklin already spoke French well, thanks to earlier classes and several trips to France with her family, but she tried to improve her mastery of the language by having conversations with this highly educated Frenchwoman. Weill soon became Franklin's friend and mentor.

By this time, Franklin had decided to specialize in physical chemistry, a field of science that combines physics and chemistry to reveal the structure and behavior of matter at the level of its atoms and molecules. When she took the second and final part of her Tripos in mid-1941, she hoped to achieve a "first"—that is, to place among the highest scorers in the test—just as she had on the first part. Unfortunately, she studied so hard that she exhausted herself and became ill, and she was still sick when she took the exams. As a result, she achieved only a high second overall. She was a top scorer in the physical chemistry examination, however, and she performed well enough in general to win a scholarship from Newnham for graduate study and a grant from the government's Department of Scientific and Industrial Research. She also obtained her bachelor's degree—or as close to a degree as she or any other woman student at the university could receive. At that time, women could earn only degrees titular from Cambridge, no matter what courses they took or how well they performed in them. This not-quite-degree was a painful reminder to Franklin that some people in the academic community still saw women as second-class citizens.

# The Holes in Coal

While war continued to rage in Europe, Rosalind Franklin fought a war of her own. Her battles were with her graduate adviser, R. G. W. Norrish (1897–1978), a renowned physical chemist who would win a share of the Nobel prize in chemistry in 1967. Norrish was going through a frustrating time in his life, and those who knew him say that he took out his feelings on the people around him, especially his graduate students and others whose junior positions left them little power to fight back.

Franklin's greatest argument with Norrish concerned her Ph.D. project, which he was supposed to assign. Most of her women friends and relatives were doing war work, ranging from aircraft manufacture to code breaking, and she would have liked a project that made some contribution to the war effort. Failing that, she wanted to work on something that would be valuable to basic science. The topic that Norrish gave her, however, seemed neither useful nor important. She also felt that her experiments would not produce the results he expected.

Franklin wrote out her objections in early 1942, but Norrish refused to read them. Used to arguing forcefully with her father and brothers when she felt she was right, she confronted him, and they had what she described to her parents as "a first-class row." She succeeded in obtaining a somewhat better assignment, but relations between the two remained stressful. (Even decades later, Norrish described her as intelligent but "stubborn and difficult to supervise.") Franklin offset the bitter taste of this relationship by spending as much time as she could with Adrienne Weill and her French refugee friends.

## STUDYING CARBON

Like other graduate students, Rosalind Franklin had been exempted from government assignment to war-related work as long as her studies continued. In 1942, however, the Ministry of Labour ruled that all women graduate students would be considered available for war assignments. Males would still be reserved.

Franklin received her assignment in August 1942. She was to be an assistant research officer with a newly formed government agency, the British Coal Utilisation Research Association (CURA). Fortunately, this placement proved to be ideal for her. Most people in the agency were around her age, and she enjoyed their spirit of informality and independence. Furthermore, Franklin knew that coal was important, not only as a fuel, but as a filter in the gas masks that Britons carried to protect themselves from a possible chemical warfare attack. Her work thus offered potential benefits to her country.

Franklin's project at CURA was to study the microstructure of different types of coal and other forms of carbon. (Coals, diamonds, and the *graphite* or "lead" in pencils are all more or less pure carbon, but the atoms in their molecules are arranged differently, so their appearance and other qualities are also very different.) In particular, she tried to learn why some kinds of carbon are much more resistant to being penetrated by gas, water, or solvents than others.

Franklin tested the ability of different types of coal to absorb molecules of helium gas at a variety of temperatures, up to 1,832°F (1,000°C). She also studied the effects of pressure and wetting. She found that coals contain microscopic openings, or pores, that vary in size according to the coal's carbon content (all coal is basically carbon, but coals can include various impurities as well). Heat and pressure make it more difficult for outside substances to reach the pores, until eventually even helium molecules—the second-smallest molecules in existence, after those of hydrogen—cannot penetrate the material. No one had studied the microscopic structure of coals in such detail before.

Franklin's work helped others predict how different kinds of coal would behave as fuels. "She brought order into a field that had previously been in chaos," Peter Hirsch, an Oxford chemist, later told Anne Sayre. Her research at CURA became her Ph.D. project, earning a degree—a real one, this time—from Cambridge in June 1945. It also produced her first scientific paper, "Thermal Expansion of Coals and Carbonised Coals," which was published in the *Transactions of the Faraday Society* in 1946.

Franklin's wartime work for the British Coal Utilisation Research Association revealed new facts about the microscopic structure of coal, which was used not only as a fuel but as a filter in gas masks like the one shown here. The coal would filter out dangerous gases that might be used in chemical warfare. *(Signal Corps Photo/National Archives)*

## LIVELY DAYS IN PARIS

World War II ended in Europe in May 1945 with the defeat of Germany and concluded completely in August 1945 after the United States dropped atomic bombs on the Japanese cities of Hiroshima and Nagasaki, forcing Japan to surrender. Franklin's required service with CURA ended in 1946, leaving her free to seek other work. She wrote half-jokingly to Adrienne Weill, who had returned to France after that country was freed from German occupation in late 1944, "If ever you hear of anybody anxious for the services of a physical chemist who knows very little about physical chemistry but a lot about the holes in coal, please let me know."

Weill did in fact have an idea in that direction. A friend of hers, Marcel Mathieu, was a senior scientist at the French government's chemical laboratory in Paris and a major power in the government agency that supported and controlled most of the scientific research done in France. When Mathieu told Weill that he planned to visit England with a fellow researcher, Jacques Mering, in fall 1946, Weill recommended that he meet with Franklin. He did so, and, impressed with Franklin's personality as well as her reputation, offered afterward to hire her as a researcher in the Paris laboratory.

Franklin was delighted to accept. Thanks partly to her time with Weill, she was already fluent in French, and she had liked the country's culture ever since her first visit there as a child. "I am quite sure I could wander happily in France for ever. I love the people, the country and the food," she wrote to her mother after a vacation there in summer 1946.

When Franklin arrived at the Laboratoire Central des Services Chimiques de l'Etat in February 1947, she found the individual culture of the "labo," as everyone called it, very welcoming as well. Many of the 14 other scientists there became her friends. The group gathered for coffee, brewed in lab flasks and served in evaporating dishes, and had lunch in nearby cafés. Some of them, including Franklin, even took their vacations together, staying at youth hostels and hiking or climbing mountains in France and Italy. Anne Sayre and Brenda Maddox, Franklin's chief biographers, agree that her years in Paris were probably the happiest of her life.

During their gatherings, the young scientists debated about nearly everything—chemistry, the social and political beliefs of the day, intellectual ideas, or books they had read. Franklin thoroughly enjoyed these vigorous discussions, which (as she wrote in one of her weekly letters to her parents) were like a game to her. She was pleased that her opinions and those of the other women were valued just as highly as the men's.

Franklin enjoyed meals at cafés and hiking vacations with fellow scientists during her years at the French government chemical laboratory in Paris. Her friend Vittorio Luzzati took this relaxed photograph of her during a hiking trip in the Alps around 1949. *(Churchill Archives Centre, Churchill College, Cambridge/reproduced with permission of Vittorio Luzzati)*

A few of Franklin's coworkers became especially important to her. One was Jacques Mering, the head of the laboratory, a somewhat older man known for his charm. "All the girls in the lab were in love with Mering," Brenda Maddox quotes one of the laboratory members as saying later, and it appears that Franklin was no exception, though her biographers differ about how deep her feelings for him went. Mering, in any case, was unavailable: Not only was he married (though he and his wife lived apart), but he had a mistress as well, another woman in the laboratory. He was fond of Franklin, however, and became her mentor and lifelong friend.

Franklin had a happier relationship with Vittorio Luzzati, a fellow scientist who lived in the same building she did. Like Franklin, Luzzati was Jewish. He had been born in Italy but left when the war began, probably to escape the persecution of Jews under the government of Fascist leader Benito Mussolini (1883–1945), an ally of Hitler's. His wife, Denise, was a medical student. The three became close friends and took at least one vacation together.

# X-RAY CRYSTALLOGRAPHY: REVEALING THE SHAPE OF MOLECULES

A few weeks after German physicist Wilhelm Roentgen (1845–1923) discovered X-rays in 1895, he was astounded to find that a photograph of his wife's hand, made by using the rays instead of light, outlined the hand's bones. Seventeen years later, another German scientist (Max von Laue [1879–1960]) and two British ones (father and son William Henry [1862–1942] and William Lawrence Bragg [1890–1971]) showed how to use the rays to—in effect—reveal the skeletons of molecules as well, something that had never been possible before.

X-rays are a form of electromagnetic radiation, just as light is, but they have a much shorter wavelength than that of visible light—about 1 *angstrom* (a unit, abbreviated A, that is defined as 0.00000000001 meter,

*(continued)*

## X-ray Crystallography

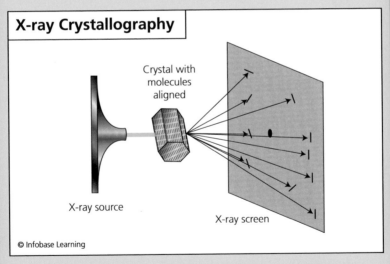

Crystal with molecules aligned

X-ray source

X-ray screen

© Infobase Learning

To make an X-ray crystallography photograph, scientists shine a narrow beam of X-rays through a crystal. The rays bounce off the atoms in the crystal, forming a pattern on an X-ray screen or sheet of photographic film that appears as black dots or streaks on a light background. The researchers measure the size, shape, and intensity of these spots and the distances between them. They then apply mathematical calculations to the measurements to work out the three-dimensional structure of the molecules in the crystal.

*(continued)*

or 0.00000000039 inch). This distance is about the same as the average distance between atoms in a molecule. When X-rays pass through a crystal, some of them strike the atoms that make up the molecules in the crystal. The atoms' electrons (subatomic particles in the atoms' outer part) diffract, or bend, the rays, creating spherical waves something like those made by pebbles thrown into a pond. Some of these waves line up with and reinforce one another, while others collide and cancel each other out. The reinforced waves strike a sheet of film beyond the crystal, producing a photograph that shows a pattern of dark spots and streaks on a light background.

To take X-ray photographs, experimenters mount a crystal in a holder, then pass a beam of rays from a special camera through it. The holder allows the crystal to be turned so that the scientists can photograph it from many angles. They measure the sizes and intensities of the black marks on the photo, as well as the distances between them. They then apply mathematical formulas to these measurements to determine the three-dimensional arrangement of the atoms inside the crystal's molecules. Computers can now perform these calculations in a few hours, but in Rosalind Franklin's day they had to be done laboriously by hand. Interpreting a single image could sometimes take a whole year.

X-ray crystallography was applied first to the crystals of simple compounds such as table salt (sodium chloride). John Desmond Bernal and a few other scientists began to use it to study complex molecules, including those in living things, in the late 1930s. Bernal worked at Cambridge during those years, but Rosalind Franklin probably did not meet him there or hear much about his research. Only later would both the man and his technique come to play important roles in her life.

## LEARNING A NEW TECHNIQUE

Franklin had realized that she would never be able to understand "the holes in coal" and other aspects of carbon's microstructure unless she learned X-ray crystallography, a technique she had heard about in Cambridge but never carried out. She could hardly have come to a better place for such training, since Jacques Mering was a crystallography expert. (Vittorio Luz-

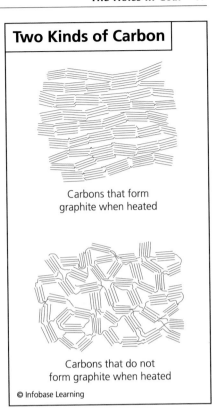

**Two Kinds of Carbon**

Carbons that form
graphite when heated

Carbons that do not
form graphite when heated

© Infobase Learning

Franklin's research in Paris led her to divide forms of carbon into two groups: those that form graphite (the substance used as the "lead" in pencils) when heated and those that do not. Graphite-forming carbons, shown at the top of this diagram, have stacks of molecules that slide easily past one another. The molecules of carbons that do not form graphite, on the other hand, form rigid structures interspersed with microscopic openings or pores. Franklin's classification proved useful in a number of industrial processes.

zati was also an X-ray crystallographer.) Mering first taught Franklin how to photograph simple crystals with X-ray beams and then how to use the procedure on carbon and other substances that did not form crystals with an orderly, repeating structure. The laboratory's X-ray apparatus required constant adjustment and cleaning, much of which Franklin did herself. Neither she nor most of the other researchers paid much attention to possible health risks from the rays, although exposure to high doses of X-rays had long been known to cause cancer.

Combining X-ray crystallography with the skills of chemical preparation that she had developed so well at CURA, Franklin continued her studies of carbon. She worked out many new details of the changes that occur in different kinds of carbon-containing substances when they are heated to high temperatures or burned. She also found that materials seemingly very unlike each other in fact sometimes had important features in common.

Eventually, Franklin divided carbon-containing substances into two groups: those that form graphite when heated and those that do not. She found that the microscopic structure of these two classes of materials differs in fundamental ways. The molecules of graphite-forming carbons are arranged in flat sheets that can easily slide past one another, but carbon-containing materials that do not form graphite have a rigid, crystal-like structure dotted with tiny holes or pores. Franklin related this difference to the chemical makeup of the substances' molecules.

Franklin's five early papers on forms of carbon "were sufficient to make a reputation had she never done anything else," Anne Sayre wrote. Her insights influenced many industrial processes, such as the making of the graphite rods that slow potentially dangerous atomic reactions in nuclear power plants. Although the main focus of Franklin's research was soon to change, she never completely lost interest in "the holes in coal"; she continued to publish papers on the structure of carbons nearly every year for the rest of her life.

## "RANDALL'S CIRCUS"

Happy as she was in Paris, Franklin began to think seriously about returning to England after several years. Her family and most of her friends were there, and her parents were pressuring her to come home. She also felt that she might find more chances to advance her career and to tackle new chemical problems if she moved to a different institution. Only a position that appealed to her strongly, however, could lure her away from France. "I shan't come home until I have a job," she wrote her parents in 1949.

In 1950, Franklin finally found a position that seemed to make leaving France worthwhile. She had sent a copy of one of her papers to Charles Coulson (1910–74), a theoretical physicist and chemist whose work she had cited in the paper. Coulson, who taught at King's College, part of the University of London, suggested that she come to King's "if you are interested in possible biological applications of the technique that you now know so well"—that is, X-ray crystallography. Franklin had never cared much about biology, but she thought that analyzing the structure of biological molecules by means of X-ray photos might present an interesting challenge.

Franklin called on Coulson during a visit to London in spring 1950, and he in turn introduced her to John Turton Randall (1905–84), head of the King's College physics department. Randall had been hailed as a war hero for coinventing a device called a cavity magnetron, which greatly increased the effectiveness of radar (*radio detection and ranging*). Radar allows aircraft to navigate and ground stations to detect approaching planes in condi-

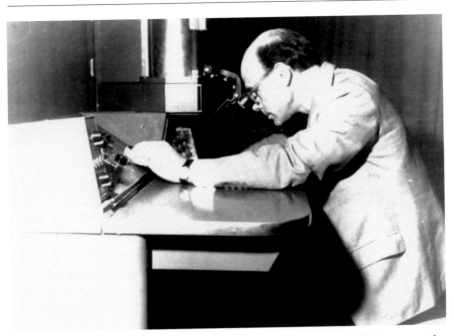

Sir John Turton Randall, shown here, was a war hero because he invented a way to improve radar, which allowed planes to fly or be detected under conditions of low visibility. When Rosalind Franklin met him in 1950, he was the director of the physics and biophysics laboratory at King's College, part of the University of London. Staff members of other laboratories at the university found the Randall group's mixture of physicists, chemists, and biologists so unusual that they nicknamed the laboratory "Randall's circus." *(King's College Archives, King's College London)*

tions of low visibility. It was a major aid to the Allies fighting Germany during World War II.

Randall's laboratory, Franklin quickly learned, was a most unusual place. Most laboratories in those days were devoted to a single branch of science, such as chemistry or physics. Randall's team, however, was a mixture of chemists, physicists, and biologists, all devoted to a single goal: trying to understand the molecules in living cells, especially those involved in passing inherited information from one generation of cells or organisms to the next. Together, they were helping to found the new discipline of *biophysics,* the application of physics to biology at the molecular level. Their interdisciplinary approach, now common in science, was then so rare that people from some of the other laboratories at the University of London called the motley group "Randall's circus."

The circus certainly did not possess an appealing tent. The biophysics laboratory was in the basement of the college's main building, three floors

King's College still showed signs of wartime damage when Franklin first saw it in 1950. This photograph shows the college as it appeared around the time of her visit. *(King's College Archives, King's College London)*

below ground. The building curved around a huge crater, 58 feet (17.7 m) long and 27 feet (8.2 m) deep, left by a wartime bomb that had landed in the middle of the college quadrangle. The scientists could still see piles of rubble left by the blast. This gloomy environment surely must have stirred Franklin's claustrophobia.

The laboratory itself intrigued Franklin, however, and Randall apparently was impressed with her as well. With his approval, she applied for an Imperial Chemical Industries (ICI) research fellowship to study in the King's College laboratory. She learned in mid-June 1950 that she had won a Turner-Newall fellowship, one of the fellowships sponsored by the ICI. The grant would cover three years of research.

Franklin was supposed to begin work at King's College that fall, but she asked for and received a postponement until the beginning of 1951. She found she was having mixed feelings about taking the job at all: "I spend half my time wondering whether to chuck the whole thing up and stay here," she wrote to her parents from Paris. In the other half of her time, however, she made careful plans for her new research, which was to be photographing proteins in solution and observing what happened as they dried out. For instance, she sent Randall a detailed description of the kind of X-ray camera she expected to need. Working in "Randall's circus," Franklin was beginning to realize, might represent the most exciting challenge she had ever faced.

# Joining the "Circus"

Rosalind Franklin did not know it, but at the same time she was preparing to join "Randall's Circus," the motley group was preparing for something new. Randall was changing the laboratory's focus from proteins to a much less well-known compound: deoxyribonucleic acid, or DNA.

A Swiss scientist, Friedrich Miescher (1844–95), had discovered DNA in 1869 when he extracted a material that he called nuclein from the central bodies, or *nuclei,* of cells. Other researchers identified a related compound, *RNA* (ribonucleic acid), in the 1920s. By 1950, when Franklin moved to King's College, scientists still were not sure what function DNA and RNA—together known as nucleic acids—carried out in living bodies. A small but growing number suspected, however, that they played some role in heredity, the transmission of characteristics from parents to children.

## INFORMATION THROUGH THE GENERATIONS

From humanity's earliest days, people noticed that the offspring of all living things usually resemble their parents. Parents with red hair are likely to have redheaded children, for instance. Offspring are not exact matches, however, so many variations of characteristics can appear. Siblings of redheaded children might be strawberry blonde or have hair of a deep chestnut brown.

Farmers and breeders took advantage of the similarity between parents and offspring, mating plants or animals with desirable characteristics, or traits, in the hope of producing large numbers of offspring with those same features. In 1859, British biologist Charles Darwin (1809–82) proposed in a groundbreaking book called *On the Origin of Species* that nature acts in the same way, allowing the living things best suited to their environments to have the most offspring. If the environment changes in a way that favors a different variation of a characteristic, generally the offspring with this particular variation will be favored. Darwin called this mechanism "evolution by natural selection."

Darwin had no idea how the information that determines traits passes from generation to generation. At the same time he was writing his book, however, an Austrian monk named Gregor Mendel (1822–84) was working on that very question by studying pea plants in his monastery garden. After breeding and observing many generations of the plants, Mendel developed simple mathematical rules by which certain characteristics appeared to be inherited. Mendel published his conclusions in an obscure journal in 1866, but his work remained virtually unknown until the beginning of the 20th century, when three biologists independently rediscovered his paper and republished it for a wider audience. As researchers verified and began to expand on Mendel's experiments, they changed the name for a unit of hereditary information, which Mendel had called a factor, to *gene*, and they named the scientific field that studies transmission of this information *genetics*.

## SEEKING THE INFORMATION CARRIER

By the time genetics was founded, biologists knew that all living things are made of microscopic units called cells. Most cells have a nucleus, and the nucleus, in turn, contains wormlike structures termed chromosomes. Cells reproduce by splitting in half, and scientists noticed that just before a cell divides, its chromosomes somehow duplicate themselves and then separate, so that one complete set goes to each daughter cell. Through breeding experiments on fruit flies, Thomas Hunt Morgan (1866–1945) and his coworkers at Columbia University in New York demonstrated in 1910 that inherited information is carried on chromosomes.

Chromosomes were found to be made up of two types of compounds: proteins and nucleic acids—in particular, DNA. Inherited (genetic) information had to be encoded in the molecules of one or the other of these substances. Most researchers thought that proteins would prove to be the carriers of this information because proteins are much more complex than nucleic acids. Both proteins and nucleic acids are long molecules made up of many smaller subunits. Proteins can have 20 common types of subunits (called *amino acids*), however, whereas nucleic acids contain only four types of subunits *(bases).*

In 1944, Oswald Avery (1877–1955), a scientist at the Rockefeller Institute for Medical Research (later Rockefeller University) in New York City,

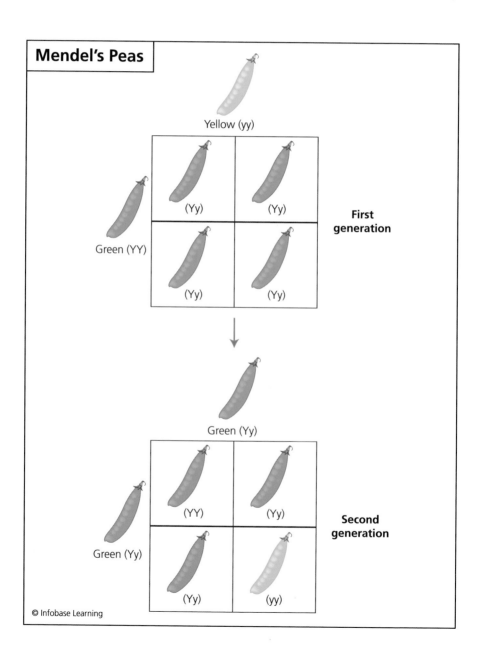

**Mendel's Peas**

Yellow (yy)

Green (YY)

(Yy)　(Yy)

(Yy)　(Yy)

**First generation**

Green (Yy)

Green (Yy)

(YY)　(Yy)

(Yy)　(yy)

**Second generation**

© Infobase Learning

and his coworkers published an account of an experiment that seemed to prove that the protein theory was wrong. Avery worked with two closely related types of bacteria, one of which was able to cause pneumonia (a serious lung disease) in laboratory animals and one of which was not. He extracted pure DNA from the disease-causing bacteria and mixed it with living germs of the type that could not cause illness. After the bacteria took up the DNA, they became able to cause pneumonia just like the other type. Their offspring also showed this characteristic.

Avery's paper, somewhat like Mendel's, was not widely read at first, and many of the scientists who did see it were not sure that they believed it. They still did not understand how such a seemingly simple molecule could transmit enough information to specify all the complex characteristics found in living things. They also did not see how it could reproduce itself so that those traits could be passed from cell to cell and organism to organism through the generations. Nonetheless, a small but growing number of researchers decided that they wanted to learn more about DNA.

Scientists had known since the beginning of the century that nucleic acids consist of three types of simpler substance: *phosphate* (a compound containing an atom of the element phosphorus surrounded by four oxygen atoms), sugar, and bases. In both DNA and RNA, one phosphate molecule, one sugar molecule, and one base join together to make up a subunit called a *nucleotide*. (DNA contains a slightly different type of sugar than RNA does, and one of the kinds of base is also different.) Nucleic acid molecules are long strings of these subunits, with the phosphate and sugar molecules alternating to form the chain and the bases attached to them. Exactly how these components were arranged within the molecule, however, remained unclear.

(*opposite page*) This diagram illustrates a basic rule of inheritance that Mendel discovered by studying pea plants. He found that some traits in the plants were more likely to appear in succeeding generations. He called the commonly seen traits dominant and the less commonly seen ones recessive. Green pods, represented here by capital Y, were a dominant trait and yellow pods (lower-case *y*) a recessive trait. Each parent contributes one "factor" (later called a gene) that governs a trait. Mendel observed that a recessive trait appears only when an offspring inherits a recessive factor from both parents. Thus, no plants in the first generation of offspring from a green-podded plant and a yellow-podded plant will have yellow pods, although all carry a factor that can produce such pods. In the second generation (offspring of two plants, each of which carries one green and one yellow factor), an average of one in every four plants will inherit a recessive yellow factor from both parents and therefore will have yellow pods.

## X-RAYING DNA

Researchers in the late 1940s were coming to realize that in the complex substances that make up the bodies of living things the structure of the compounds' molecules is intimately related to the substances' function. Scientists therefore could not fully understand how these chemicals work until they learned their molecular structure. As Rosalind Franklin had found out in France, new techniques were beginning to allow X-ray crystallography to be applied to molecules that do not form regular crystals, including the molecules of compounds found in living things. This technology was proving to be one of the best ways to determine the structure of complicated molecules.

In the late 1930s, while Rosalind Franklin was studying at Cambridge, John Desmond Bernal at that university and another British scientist William Astbury (1889–1961) of the University of Leeds took the first X-ray photographs of DNA. Astbury stated in a 1938 paper that the molecule probably had the overall form of a *helix,* a twisted shape like a corkscrew, with the phosphates and sugars making up the screw shape and the bases projecting from them. He believed that the bases lay flat and were stacked like plates inside the molecule, separated by a distance of 3.4 angstroms. Astbury's X-ray pictures were fuzzy, however, and they did not show clearly whether his guesses about the DNA molecule were correct.

In order to take better X-ray photographs of DNA, scientists needed purer samples of the compound than were usually available. In May 1950, shortly after Franklin took her first look at "Randall's circus," a Swiss scientist named Rudolf Signer (1903–90) told a meeting of Britain's Faraday Society that he had found a way to prepare the nucleic acid so it could be stretched into long, thin fibers like the threads of a spider web. The standard methods of extracting DNA from animal cells did not produce such fibers. Signer offered samples of his jellylike DNA to any scientists at the meeting who wanted to study it.

One of the researchers who left with a test tube of Signer's gel was Maurice Wilkins, a former physicist who was then the assistant director of Randall's laboratory. Wilkins had been born in New Zealand, but he was raised in England and had earned his Ph.D. from Cambridge. During World War II, he worked in the United States on the Manhattan Project, the research that developed the atomic bomb. Repelled by the destruction that the bomb caused, he returned to Britain after the war and turned away from pure physics to seek "a new world of science where . . . physics interacted with the biology of living things," as he put it in his autobiography, *The Third Man of the Double Helix.* He worked with Randall at St. Andrews, a university in Scotland, and then moved with him to King's College. Wilkins's specialty was inventing new types of microscopes and using them to study living cells.

New Zealand–born Maurice Wilkins, shown here with an X-ray machine in 1955, had begun taking X-ray photographs of DNA shortly before Rosalind Franklin arrived at King's College in 1951. He expected her to work as his assistant on the project, but Franklin's own expectations were quite different. *(National Library of Medicine)*

Beginning around 1947, Wilkins had examined DNA in cells with reflecting microscopes that used ultraviolet light. At first, he intended to continue this work with Signer's DNA, but then he noticed that the fibers from the sample showed a well-ordered appearance under a microscope in polarized light (light in which all the waves are aligned in the same plane, as opposed to being aligned randomly as they are in normal light). This suggested that the fibers contained long molecules lying parallel to each other, the best kind of arrangement for X-ray photography. Wilkins therefore decided to apply X-ray crystallography to the material instead.

Wilkins himself had never taken photos with an X-ray camera, so he enlisted the help of Raymond Gosling (1926–   ), a newly arrived graduate student who was already using this technique to examine the DNA in sperm as part of his Ph.D. project. The two had only an old war-era camera, so they jury-rigged the rest of their equipment from whatever materials they could find. For instance, when they detected a leak in the tube through which the X-rays entered the camera, they sealed it with a condom. Following a suggestion from Randall, they filled the camera with hydrogen gas rather than air so that the X-ray beam would not be scattered by the air molecules.

Even with this patched-together gear, Wilkins and Gosling were soon producing photos far better than any Astbury had taken. The spots on the photographs formed a clear X shape, which proved that DNA could indeed form crystals. Regularly spaced blank spots along the length of the X suggested to another laboratory member, physicist Alec Stokes, that Astbury had been right to think that the DNA molecule was a helix. This idea fitted with the fact that chromosomes themselves have a spiral or helical shape.

## A CONFUSING LETTER

John Randall had told Wilkins that Rosalind Franklin was going to join the King's College biophysics laboratory, and since Franklin was an expert on X-ray crystallography, Wilkins suggested that she be added to the team working on DNA rather than pursuing her original assignment of photographing proteins. Randall agreed. In early December 1950, he wrote to Franklin:

> [I]t would be a good deal more important for you to investigate the structure of certain biological fibres in which we are interested, both by low and high angle diffraction, rather than to continue with the original project of work on solutions. . . . [A]s far as the experimental X-ray effort is concerned

there will be at the moment only yourself and [Raymond] Gosling. . . . Gosling, working in conjunction with Wilkins, has already found that fibres of desoxyribose nucleic acid derived from material provided by Professor Signer of Berne give remarkably good fibre diagrams.

Rosalind Franklin began working at the King's College laboratory on January 5, 1951—and trouble erupted almost immediately. Part of it, Franklin's biographers and Maurice Wilkins later agreed, was John Randall's fault. As Randall's "right-hand man" (as Wilkins put it) and head of the ongoing DNA project, Wilkins had good reason to expect that any new scientist assigned to that project would be working more or less under his supervision. Randall never told him otherwise—but Randall's letter to Franklin, which Wilkins did not see, had failed to mention Wilkins at all. Instead, it stated that Franklin and Gosling would work alone on the DNA X-ray research. Such independence seemed quite logical to Franklin, since she was by then an experienced and respected scientist. No one knows exactly why Randall sent such conflicting messages, but there is no doubt that the confusion he created had fateful consequences.

The fact that Wilkins was on vacation when Randall introduced Franklin to the rest of the laboratory staff did not help the situation. He therefore was not present to object when Randall made statements at the meeting that reinforced what he had written in his letter. Raymond Gosling later told science historian Horace Freeland Judson, author of a book about early DNA research called *The Eighth Day of Creation*:

I was in no doubt that what Randall was saying was that here was the problem, here was a research student [that is, Gosling himself] . . . here were the X-ray photographs, . . . get some more, and solve the structure of DNA from the X-ray diffraction pattern. And that's what Rosalind from then on tried to do.

When Wilkins returned, he was understandably shocked to find that the new arrival had seemingly taken over his work on DNA. Sharon McGrayne, author of *Nobel Prize Women in Science*, quotes Gosling as saying, "I don't think Wilkins ever imagined that giving a problem to Rosalind meant that nobody else was going to work on it. The lab wasn't built like that, but Rosalind was built like that." Franklin, for her part, could not understand why Wilkins was trying to involve himself in a project that she thought he had turned over to her.

# PERSONALITY CLASH

The problem created by Randall's contradictory instructions was made worse by the fact that Franklin and Wilkins's personalities clashed—ultimately so strongly that Horace Judson called the conflict between them "one of the great personal quarrels in the history of science." The contrasts did not show immediately because the two had a number of things in common. Both were Cambridge graduates, for instance, and they shared, as Wilkins wrote in his autobiography, "broad interests in education, culture and social justice." Their differences, however, soon far outweighed these similarities.

One of those differences was in social class. Although Franklin never spoke of her family's money, Jean Hanson, the group's senior biologist, told Brenda Maddox that Franklin "looked like an aristocrat and . . . acted like one." Franklin, in turn, perceived Wilkins and many of the other laboratory members—with disapproval—as "so middle class," as she wrote to her old friend Vittorio Luzzati.

Far more important was their difference in temperament. Franklin was a forthright person, used to saying exactly what she thought. She had always enjoyed arguing, first with her father and later with her French colleagues. It was a kind of sport to her, something to pursue vigorously with no hard feelings afterward. As Raymond Gosling told Anne Sayre:

> If you believed what you were saying, you had to argue strongly with Rosalind if she thought you were wrong. . . . Rosalind always wanted to justify herself, or, if she was discussing with me, she always expected me to justify myself very strongly indeed. . . . She didn't suffer fools gladly at all. You either had to be on the ball, or you were lost in any discussion [with her].

Wilkins, by contrast, was shy and hated conflict. He found Franklin abrupt, cold, and intimidating. To him she seemed, as he later said to Sayre, "very fierce. . . . She denounced, and this made it quite impossible as far as I was concerned to have a civil conversation. I simply had to walk away." That was the worst possible approach to take with Franklin, who mistook his lack of combativeness for a lack of intelligence.

# VICTIM OF DISCRIMINATION?

To Anne Sayre and some later writers, the most important contrast of all between Franklin and Wilkins was their difference in gender. These writers have blamed most of Franklin's difficulties at King's College on the fact that she was a woman, in an era when women scientists were still rare and were often the targets of discrimination.

The college certainly possessed a few rules that institutionalized discrimination. Women were not allowed to eat in Kings's senior common room, for example. Sayre thought this exclusion deprived Franklin of the shared time with colleagues that often plays such an important part in science. However, another friend of Franklin's, Anne Piper, wrote in a memoir article about Franklin published in *Trends in Biochemical Sciences* in 1998 that Franklin told her the ban was "just stupid." Brenda Maddox points out that the college's other dining room, which women and men could share, served the same food, and many of the men preferred it to the male-only room.

Far more important was the status of women in Randall's laboratory itself. Sayre claimed that only one other woman worked in the "circus" during Franklin's stay there, but both Brenda Maddox and Horace Judson say that the laboratory staff of 31 included at least eight women, some of whom held high positions. This was a greater proportion of women than most laboratories of the time possessed. Judson communicated with seven of these women in the late 1970s, and he reported that all "agreed that women at their laboratory were treated equitably" in Franklin's time. If Franklin was isolated, several said, it was by her own choice. For instance, a laboratory scientist named Mary Fraser told Judson:

> Informal coffee get-togethers were the accepted form of social gathering [for lab members]. . . . I suppose we assumed [that Franklin] would fit into the casual role of relaxing amidst the beakers, balances, centrifuges and petri dishes—but she didn't. Rosalind didn't seem to want to mix.

Part of the problem, biographies of Franklin have shown, was that there were "two Rosalinds." Throughout Franklin's life, most—though not all—of her coworkers saw only the austere, dedicated scientist who frightened Wilkins so badly and repelled some of her laboratory mates. Only those whom Franklin liked and trusted saw the other Rosalind, the lively woman who had so charmed her colleagues in Paris. During her years at King's College, Franklin apparently reserved this side of herself almost exclusively for family and old friends whom she saw outside the laboratory. She went to the theater or movies with them, played with their children (whose company she always enjoyed), or entertained them with home-cooked gourmet dinners (with French recipes, of

## *WHAT IS LIFE?*: A FAR-REACHING BOOK

One of the most influential books in mid-20th-century biology, Erwin Schrödinger's *What Is Life?*, was written by a physicist. This small volume helped to launch the new field of *molecular biology*, which investigates biological processes by studying the structure and function of the complex molecules in the bodies of living things.

Schrödinger (1887–1961) was born in Austria but spent the first part of his career in Germany. He was already famous when *What Is Life?* was published in 1944 because he had helped to found another new field, quantum physics or *quantum mechanics*, in the 1920s. Quantum mechanics studies the behavior of atoms and the particles of which atoms are made.

Schrödinger left Germany in 1933, when the Nazi government came into power, because he disliked the government's anti-Semitism, even though he himself was not a Jew. After teaching at a number of universities in Europe, the United States, and the British Isles, he finally moved to Dublin, Ireland, in 1940 and became an Irish citizen. *What Is Life?* was based on a series of lectures he gave in February 1943 at the Dublin Institute for Advanced Studies.

*What Is Life?* presented two extremely influential ideas. The first was that applying the principles of chemistry and physics to biology would lead to exciting new discoveries. This approach led a number of physi-

course) in her new apartment. At these gatherings, Brenda Maddox writes, she was an "amusing conversationalist and attentive hostess."

## YOUNG GENIUS

Retreating to a separate room in the King's College laboratory, Franklin and Raymond Gosling, whose Ph.D. research she was now supervising, set to work improving their X-ray equipment. Franklin ordered a vacuum pump to extract air from the camera interior more efficiently, for instance. She also began working with Gosling to design a platform that would let the camera tilt so they could photograph the DNA fibers from different angles.

cists to develop an interest in biology for the first time. The second was Schrödinger's recommendation that the gene—whose physical nature was not yet known—be studied as a molecule and as a carrier of information. He believed that the genetic molecule, whatever it would prove to be, would form crystals, but the molecules in these crystals would not be arranged in a the sort of repeating structure that crystals of simpler substances possessed. Variations in the molecules and the bonds between them, Schrödinger predicted, would somehow encode the inherited information that shapes the characteristics of living things. He pointed out that Morse code, which has only two symbols (dot and dash), can be made to spell out any word by combining the symbols in groups of four or fewer and using these combinations to stand for letters in the alphabet.

Rosalind Franklin did not read *What Is Life?*, but three of the other scientists closely involved in determining the structure of DNA—James Watson, Francis Crick, and Maurice Wilkins—did. For all three of these men, and a number of other researchers as well, the book produced a life-altering experience. Wilkins and Crick wrote in their autobiographies that they changed their research focus from physics to biology partly because of it, and Watson, who read the book when he was only 17, credits it in his memoir as his inspiration to discover what genes really are. If Schrödinger had not written this book, the discovery of DNA's structure might have been delayed for many years.

Randall's laboratory had just acquired a fine-focus X-ray tube that aligned the rays in a very narrow beam, producing sharper pictures than the old tube. Fitted with a very small camera, this new tube was expected to be able to photograph a single DNA fiber, 0.004 inch (0.1 mm) across, rather than the groups of fibers Wilkins and Gosling had been using. The small camera also helped Franklin and Gosling control the humidity (degree of dampness) inside the camera's chamber, which was important because incorporating water molecules into the DNA fiber affected its structure.

Maurice Wilkins, meanwhile, took a break from the King's College laboratory by attending a scientific conference on large molecules at the Marine Biological Station in Naples, Italy, in May 1951. During this conference, he

As a graduate student, Raymond Gosling helped Rosalind Franklin take fine X-ray photographs of DNA and analyze them at King's College. Gosling spent most of his later career at the medical school of Guy's Hospital, a venerable London hospital, where he showed students how physics could be applied to medicine and developed ultrasound devices to be used on blood vessels. *(King's College Archives, King's College London)*

gave a lecture explaining why he and his coworkers were focusing on DNA. He presented some of the X-ray photographs he and Gosling had made, and he offered evidence that the features of extracted DNA shown in the photographs would also be found in the DNA of living cells. He added that other members of his laboratory were preparing to make photos that would reveal even more about the DNA molecule's structure.

One member of the audience hearing Wilkins's lecture was a gawky young American named James Dewey Watson. Watson was only 23 years old, but he had already earned his Ph.D. from the University of Indiana. He had become fascinated by genes and inheritance as a senior at the University of Chicago, and he knew about Oswald Avery's suggestion that nucleic acids held the key to this mystery. Watson's work as a graduate student had focused on the genetics of viruses, but he had decided that the secret of genes' ability to duplicate themselves lay in their chemical structure, and this was what he really wanted to study. He had been doing postdoctoral work on the biochemistry of nucleic acids in Copenhagen, but he found that project disappointing because it had nothing to do with genes.

Watson was thrilled to hear that DNA could be prepared in a crystalline form and analyzed with X-rays. This meant that the DNA molecule had a regular, repeating structure that could be "solved in a straightforward fashion," as he wrote later in *The Double Helix*, rather than being "fantastically irregular," as many protein molecules were. Watson knew nothing about the techniques of X-ray crystallography, but if he could not analyze DNA in that way himself, he determined to find someone else who could. He tried to persuade Wilkins to let him join the King's College laboratory, but he was unsuccessful.

## "HELICES WERE IN THE AIR"

Maurice Wilkins repeated his Naples talk at an informal conference at Cambridge's Cavendish Laboratory in July. Some of the scientists there were interested in his work because they were following a parallel path, using X-ray crystallography to investigate the structure of protein molecules. One of these researchers, Francis Harry Compton Crick, was an old friend of Wilkins's; they had met shortly after the war when Crick attempted to obtain a position at King's College. Like Wilkins, Crick was a physicist who had transferred to biology, teaching himself, among other things, X-ray crystallography. Crick, the opposite of the precocious James Watson, was 35 years old at the time of Wilkins's lecture but had not yet earned his doctor's degree because his war service had delayed the completion of his schooling. At the moment, he was trying to work out the molecular structure of *hemoglobin*, the iron-containing substance that makes blood red and carries oxygen throughout the body.

Crick might have been impressed by Wilkins's lecture, but Rosalind Franklin, who also attended it, apparently was not. As Wilkins left the Cambridge laboratory, she met him outside and told him firmly that he should stop discussing X-ray work on DNA. That project, she felt, now belonged to her. "Go back to your microscopes!" she snapped. As Wilkins wrote later in *The Third Man of the Double Helix,* he was "shocked and bewildered" at Franklin's demand—and irritated as well, since in fact he was more interested in pursuing the crystallography work than ever.

Scientists that summer were buzzing about an exciting discovery that United States chemist Linus Pauling (1901–94) had just announced: protein molecules have the shape of a helix. It seemed quite possible, therefore, that other important biological molecules, including nucleic acids, might have this form as well. As Francis Crick later said (quoted in Brenda Maddox's book), "Helices [pl.] were in the air."

They certainly were on the mind of Maurice Wilkins. Soon after reading a paper in which Pauling described the protein helix, Wilkins asked another member of the King's College laboratory, physicist Alec Stokes, to determine mathematically what sort of X-ray pattern a molecule shaped like a helix would have. Stokes did so. Now Wilkins knew what the X-ray version of a helix would look like—but he did not know whether that was what Rosalind Franklin's pictures would show.

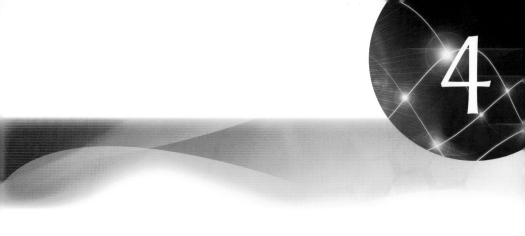

# Funeral for a Helix

By September 1951, Rosalind Franklin and Raymond Gosling had finished preparing their equipment and were finally ready to begin making their X-ray pictures of DNA. Before taking each set of photographs, they stuck a needle in Signer's gel and slowly pulled it out, producing a slender fiber in which the DNA molecules were aligned lengthwise. They mounted this fiber inside their small camera, then added water a little at a time by bubbling hydrogen gas through salt solutions of known humidities and letting the gas flow into the camera chamber. This technique worked much better than the version Wilkins had used, a fact that Franklin emphasized with what Wilkins in his autobiography called a "very superior attitude."

## TWO FORMS OF DNA

Franklin and Gosling quickly made an important discovery: DNA existed in two forms. One, which they called the *A,* or "dry," *form,* was crystalline and appeared at fairly low (75 percent) relative humidity. The other—the *B,* or "wet," *form*—was more fibrous and could be seen only at high humidity (90 percent). The DNA could be made to alternate between the two forms simply by changing the humidity. The fiber became much longer and thinner when it went from the dry form to the wet, switching so abruptly that the lengthening fiber sometimes popped off the stand that held it in place inside the X-ray camera. Franklin concluded that the photographs taken by Astbury

## A and B Forms of DNA

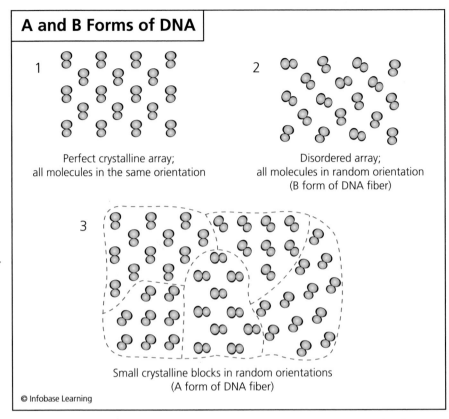

1

Perfect crystalline array;
all molecules in the same orientation

2

Disordered array;
all molecules in random orientation
(B form of DNA fiber)

3

Small crystalline blocks in random orientations
(A form of DNA fiber)

© Infobase Learning

Soon after Rosalind Franklin and Raymond Gosling began making X-ray photographs of DNA at different humidities, they found that DNA exists in two forms that produce different kinds of photographs because their molecules are arranged in different ways. In classic crystals—the kind of solids on which X-ray crystallography was first used—all the molecules have the same orientation (1). By contrast, the molecules in the B (wet) form of DNA, which appears only in conditions of high humidity, are randomly oriented (2). The A (dry) form of DNA is somewhere between the two; all the molecules in a small block of the material have the same orientation, but the orientations in two adjoining blocks are likely to be different (3).

and other early researchers had been blurry because the scientists unknowingly had been working with a mixture of the two forms.

Wilkins proposed to Franklin that they collaborate to study the two forms of DNA, but she brusquely rejected his offer. In late October, trying to keep peace, Randall told them to divide the work. Franklin, using the Signer DNA and the small camera, was to concentrate on the A form, which acted more like a crystal than the B form and therefore seemed likely to give sharper reflections of the X-ray beam. Wilkins, meanwhile, was to study the

B form, using less pure DNA from another source and his old X-ray camera. Wilkins agreed to the decision, but he soon discovered that his DNA sample was far inferior to the Signer DNA and did not show the transition between the A and B forms. He eventually gave up on it and returned to making X-ray photos of DNA in the sperm of squid, a marine animal.

Shortly after Randall's decision, Wilkins pointed out to Franklin that her earlier photographs of the B form of DNA showed exactly the X-ray diffraction characteristics that Alec Stokes had predicted for a molecule with a helix shape. He wrote in his autobiography that his comment made Franklin furious, apparently because she saw it as another attempt to intrude on her work. In fact, however, Anne Sayre writes that Franklin agreed with Wilkins that the DNA molecule would prove to be a helix, made up of one or several chains. She believed that the phosphates were on the outside of the chains because these molecules attract water, and water clearly moved in and out of the DNA fiber easily as the humidity changed. The bases would be on the inside, she thought, lying perpendicular to the phosphate-sugar chains and linked to one another by hydrogen bonds.

## CONFRONTATION AND COLLABORATION

The tension in the King's College laboratory was wearing Franklin down as much as it was Wilkins. By October 1951, less than a year after her arrival, she was already thinking of leaving the group. "I . . . want to get out as soon as possible," she wrote to Adrienne Weill. She felt isolated, she said, because "King's has neither foreigners nor Jews" (a belief that Brenda Maddox claims was incorrect). She also had concluded that few members of the laboratory staff could meet the high standards she set for herself and those around her:

> The very young are mostly thoroughly nice but none of them brilliant. . . . [Most of the] middle and senior people are positively repulsive. . . . There isn't a first-class or even a good brain among them . . . nobody with whom I particularly want to discuss anything, scientific or otherwise. . . . I so much prefer to work under somebody who commands my respect and can offer some encouragement.

Wilkins, meanwhile, began paying frequent visits to his old friend Francis Crick in Cambridge. They talked about the research going on at King's as well as Wilkins's other favorite subject, the difficulty of getting along with

Rosalind Franklin. Her refusal to discuss her data made him feel shut out of the project that he himself had begun, he complained. It also conflicted with his belief that scientists should be open with one another and share their findings.

Crick was not the only one who listened to Wilkins's tales of woe. They also filled the eager ears of Crick's new coworker, James Watson, who had arranged to be transferred to the Cavendish Laboratory in October so he could learn how to use X-ray crystallography to work out the structure of large biological molecules.

Watson and Crick had scientific and personal backgrounds as different as those of Franklin and Wilkins, but in this case the opposites attracted, and the two quickly became close friends. At the Cavendish, Watson later wrote in his memoir, *The Double Helix,* "I . . . immediately discovered the fun of talking to Francis Crick." Crick, for his part, wrote in *What Mad Pursuit,* his autobiography, "Jim and I hit it off immediately, partly because our interests were astonishingly similar and partly, I suspect, because a certain youthful arrogance, a ruthlessness, and an impatience with sloppy thinking came naturally to both of us."

As the best collaborators do, the pair pooled their scientific expertise. Watson taught Crick about genetics, and Crick, in turn, tutored Watson in X-ray crystallography. They talked together constantly, not only in their shared office at the Cavendish but on strolls through the Backs (the gardens that lie between the colleges of Cambridge and the river Cam) and in the Eagle, a nearby pub where they often ate lunch. Their favorite subject was DNA, which Watson had already come to think of as "the most golden of all molecules." Watson believed that unraveling the nucleic acid's secrets would be a sure path, not only to important scientific knowledge, but to fame—perhaps even to the highest of scientific honors, the Nobel Prize.

## A CRUCIAL TALK

James Watson had a chance to see Wilkins's nemesis for himself on November 21, when he attended a colloquium on nucleic acid structure that was held at King's College. Rosalind Franklin spoke last at the meeting, following Wilkins and Alec Stokes. She described the A and B forms of DNA and explained what she and Gosling had learned about them so far. Her notes for this talk, which were found later among her papers, refer to the likelihood that the DNA molecule had a helical shape, but neither Wilkins nor Watson remembered her mentioning that possibility in the talk itself.

# MODEL BUILDING: THREE-DIMENSIONAL CHEMISTRY

Linus Pauling and his coworker Robert Corey (1897–1971) essentially invented *model building* as a tool for working out the structure of complex molecules, and Pauling used it brilliantly to work out the basic structure of proteins. This approach allows a scientist to combine data obtained from a variety of fields, such as X-ray crystallography and biochemistry, into a single three-dimensional picture.

Building models might seem like mere play, but the process is supported by hard science. Researchers construct the parts of the model to an exact scale, based on calculation of the sizes of individual atoms and the bonds between them. In connecting these pieces, a researcher must keep in mind the rules that physics lays down for the ways in which atoms within molecules can combine. They can join one another at some angles and distances but not at others, and the rules are different for different kinds of atoms and kinds of chemical bonds. Knowledge of these constraints limits scientists' choices in assembling the model. "The essential trick" of model-building, James Watson wrote in *The Double Helix*, "was to ask which atoms like to sit next to each other."

The completed model must fit with the data about the molecule that X-ray crystallography has provided. Some scientists rely on X-ray data more than others in constructing their models, however. Francis Crick preferred to use as little data as possible while constructing models. In *The Eighth Day of Creation*, Horace Judson explained this approach as follows:

> The sport would be to see how little data [Crick and Watson] could make do with and still get it right. . . . Crick, following Pauling, elevated this penurious elegance into a theoretical principle, the corollary of model building. . . . Crick said, "There's a perfectly sound reason . . . why you should use the *minimum* of experimental data. . . . Evidence can be unreliable, and therefore you should use as little of it as you can."

On the other hand, Aaron Klug wrote in his article about the discovery of DNA in Torsten Krude's *DNA: Changing Science and Society*, "The more detailed the [X-ray data] is, the better the chance of [the model's] succeeding."

Watson took no notes during Franklin's talk, as was his habit. Indeed, according to his account in *The Double Helix,* he was more interested in critiquing the woman scientist's appearance than in paying attention to her words: "I wondered how she would look if she took off her glasses and did something novel with her hair." This description, written many years after the event, has both amused and angered Franklin's biographers, who point out that she never wore glasses.

Relying on that same less-than-precise memory, Watson described the seminar to Crick after he returned to Cambridge. His accuracy was reduced further by the fact that, in spite of Crick's tutoring, he did not really understand the technical terms that X-ray crystallographers used. Much of what Franklin had said, therefore, was beyond his grasp, and he remembered it either incorrectly or not at all.

Nonetheless, Watson and Crick hoped that they now had enough information to make their first attempt to solve the DNA molecule's structure. They planned to use the same technique that Linus Pauling had applied so successfully to the structure of proteins: building models. These stick-and-ball constructions might look like children's toys, but in the right hands, the Cambridge scientists knew, they could be powerful tools for visualizing complex shapes in three dimensions.

## TWO APPROACHES TO SCIENCE

Watson and Crick completed their model in about a week, then invited the King's College scientists to come and see it. It was a helix containing three chains, or "backbones," of sugar and phosphate, spiraling around in parallel. On the outside of the molecule, the bases extended from the chains.

Rosalind Franklin lost no time in telling Watson and Crick that their model molecule would not hold together. They had not taken into account the water molecules that would attach themselves to the DNA. She explained that the phosphate groups had to be on the outside of the DNA molecule so they could attract and hold the water, as DNA was known to do. The two men realized she was correct: Watson had remembered the wrong figure for the amount of water in the molecule and had passed that error on to Crick.

Franklin, in fact, thought the whole idea of model building was foolish, at least when the models were based on as little factual information as was currently available for DNA. Under those circumstances, she felt, it was too hard to tell whether a model was really correct—whether it was, as she was fond of saying, "*the* solution or *a* solution." A deeper reason for her disapproval was that model building represented the exact opposite of the way that she preferred to approach scientific problems.

Some scientists like to use *deductive reasoning,* in which they make imaginative leaps to guess the explanation for events in nature and then test their ideas against evidence from experiments. Others take the opposite, or *inductive,* approach, in which they painstakingly collect experimental data and use that information to build up a picture of the phenomenon they are studying. Many researchers alternate between these two methods, but some use one or the other most of the time.

Rosalind Franklin was almost purely an inductive scientist, insisting throughout her life that the evidence should tell a researcher what to think. Theories that did not grow directly out of experimental results, she believed, were very likely to be wrong. She felt that model building, if done at all, should be carried out only after as much X-ray data as possible had been obtained. Raymond Gosling told Horace Judson that Franklin's attitude was, "'We are not going to speculate, we are going to wait, we are going to let the spots on this photograph tell us what the structure is." Watson and Crick, by contrast, believed in the deductive approach. They preferred to theorize, then check their ideas against known experimental data.

## ANALYZING DNA

Word of Watson and Crick's spectacular failure reached pioneer crystallographer Lawrence Bragg, who at that time headed the Cavendish Laboratory. He had not been happy to hear that the two men were working on DNA at all, since they were supposed to be studying proteins. Furthermore, DNA research was assumed to "belong" to King's College. Funding for scientific projects was scarce in Britain's depressed postwar economy, so laboratories at different universities usually agreed not to investigate the same subjects in order to avoid wasting resources by duplicating one another's efforts. Bragg therefore ordered Watson and Crick to stop studying DNA. Crick reluctantly returned to his research on hemoglobin, and Watson began to study the other nucleic acid, RNA, in tobacco mosaic virus. The two never stopped thinking about their favorite molecule, however.

More eager to escape King's than ever, Rosalind Franklin visited Paris during the Christmas vacation in 1951 to ask whether the government laboratory would take her back, but Jacques Mering refused to do so; according to Brenda Maddox, he was uninterested in rehiring anyone who had left his laboratory. On her return, therefore, she asked expert crystallographer J. D.

Bernal for permission to transfer to his laboratory at Birkbeck, another of the colleges at the University of London. Bernal said that he would be delighted to have her whenever Randall was willing to let her go.

Back in her laboratory, following a suggestion that her old friend Vittorio Luzzati had made when she saw him in France, Franklin prepared to apply a set of mathematical formulas called *Patterson functions* to her X-ray photos of the A form of DNA. Modern computers can make the Patterson calculations in just a few minutes, but Franklin and Gosling knew they would have to spend many tedious hours with pencil, paper, and adding machine to obtain the results they needed. Nonetheless, Franklin believed that these calculations would provide the most accurate picture of the DNA molecule's three-dimensional structure. True to her inductive nature, she trusted the Patterson functions because they did not require making any assumptions about the molecule.

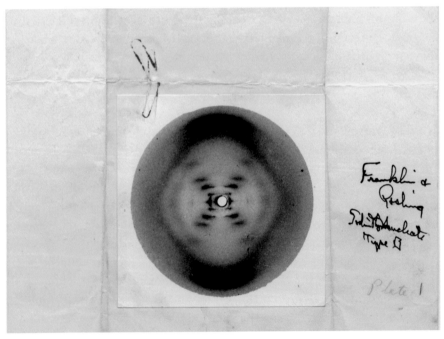

The X-shaped pattern that dominates this X-ray photograph of the B form of DNA, which Rosalind Franklin took in May 1952 and labeled Photo 51, shows clearly that the molecules in this form must have a helix shape. This and other features of the photograph were a revelation to James Watson when Maurice Wilkins showed it to him (without Franklin's permission) in January 1953. They provided clues that helped Watson and Crick determine the structure of the DNA molecule. *(From Ava Helen and Linus Pauling Papers, Special Collections, Oregon State University)*

On May 1, 1952, Franklin made what proved to be the best DNA photograph she ever took. Clear X-ray photos often require very long exposures, and this one needed 100 hours. Although most of her research had been devoted to the A form of the molecule, this photo was of a single fiber in the B, or "wet," form. Its X shape of black stripes, with no marks between the arms of the X, showed very clearly that this form of the DNA molecule had to be a helix. That did not surprise Franklin, who had always believed that the B form possessed this shape. She labeled the photo "No. 51," then set it aside and went back to her work on the A form.

## DEATH NOTICE

The B form of DNA might be a helix, but Franklin had her doubts about whether this was true of the A form. She found several signs in her photos of this form that, to her eye, ruled out a helical structure. When she described these findings to Francis Crick during a chance meeting in early 1952, he told her that she was mistaken. Her data, he said, could be explained in a way that would permit a helix after all. Unfortunately, he spoke (as he later admitted in his autobiography) in a condescending tone that angered Franklin, and she refused to believe him.

Franklin's Patterson calculations seemed to be pointing in the same direction as her direct interpretation of the photographs. In July, therefore, after months of work, she decided that the molecular shape of DNA's A form could not be a helix. As a humorous way of telling the other laboratory members about this conclusion, she and Gosling passed out little black-bordered cards to everyone on July 18. The cards read:

> It is with great regret that we have to announce the death, on Friday 18th July 1952 of D.N.A. helix (crystalline)
> Death followed a protracted illness. . . .
> A memorial service will be held next Monday or Tuesday.
> It is hoped that Dr. M. H. F. Wilkins will speak in memory of the late helix.
> > R. E. Franklin, R. Gosling.

At the "memorial service," Franklin spread out her Patterson equations and photographs of the A form for everyone to see. Wilkins was neither amused nor impressed, but he could find no reason to doubt the evidence that she had so painstakingly gathered. As a result, he too began to question the idea that the DNA molecule could be a helix, which had seemed so clear to him before.

Franklin could have handed out a "death notice" for her stay in the King's College laboratory at the same time. She had told Randall in June that she wanted to move to Birkbeck, and Randall had speedily agreed; indeed, he may have been relieved to see one of the warring parties leaving his "circus." The move was scheduled for the beginning of 1953.

# The Race

The race to solve the structure of DNA began in earnest in January 1953—or so, at least, James Watson saw it. (Francis Crick told Horace Freeland Judson, "The only person who thought it was a race was Jim.") Peter Pauling (1931–2003), Linus Pauling's son, fired the starting gun. Pauling, who had joined the Cavendish Laboratory the previous August, shared an office with Watson and Crick. In mid-December, he told them about a letter he had just received from his father in which the eminent chemist said he believed that he and Robert Corey had worked out the structure of the DNA molecule.

Watson was determined not to be "scooped." If he and Crick could find the structure themselves before Linus Pauling published a paper about his discovery, he thought they might still have a chance to win the acclaim that Watson was sure awaited the person who revealed the shape of the "golden molecule."

## SIX WEEKS OF BREATHING ROOM

Rosalind Franklin, back at King's College, had no idea that she was participating in a contest. She was simply hurrying to complete and write up her DNA research before her eagerly awaited transfer to Birkbeck in March. (The date of Franklin's departure had been delayed from January because she had lost a month of work time from an attack of influenza.) She was working on three papers, all to be coauthored with Raymond Gosling. One described the two forms of DNA they had discovered and the conditions under which one

# LINUS PAULING: WIDE-RANGING GENIUS

Linus Carl Pauling is the only person to win two unshared Nobel Prizes. He made major contributions to physics, chemistry, biology, and medicine—and, even more important, to fields that combine these sciences, such as quantum chemistry (in which quantum mechanics is applied to chemistry—a discipline he helped to found) and molecular biology.

Pauling was born in Portland, Oregon, on February 28, 1901. He quit high school shortly before graduation and enrolled in Oregon Agricultural College, now Oregon State University, at age 16. He earned a bachelor of science degree in chemical engineering from the college in 1922.

Pauling's interests soon turned from engineering to basic science, focusing on the questions of how atoms join together to form molecules and how the structure of molecules affects their qualities, or properties. He did graduate work at the California Institute of Technology (Caltech), located in Pasadena, and earned his Ph.D. in physical chemistry and mathematical physics from that institution in 1925. He

Linus Pauling made fundamental discoveries in physics, chemistry, and medicine and won two unshared Nobel Prizes, one in chemistry in 1954 for his work on chemical bonds and one in peace in 1962 for political activism that helped to bring about a treaty banning aboveground testing of nuclear weapons. Scientists did not accept all of his ideas, however. His proposed structure for the DNA molecule proved to be a failure because he made a simple mistake in chemistry. (*Library of Congress*)

then went to Europe, where he learned about the new field of quantum mechanics and began to think of ways to apply its insights to chemistry.

On his return to the United States in 1927, Pauling joined the faculty of Caltech, and by 1937 he was chairman of the university's chemistry department. His first major contribution to science was *The Nature of the Chemical Bond*, which explains how atoms join together to form molecules. Scientists still refer to this book, published in 1939. Pauling's first Nobel Prize, the chemistry prize for 1954, was awarded primarily for this work.

Pauling had worked primarily with simple molecules in his research on chemical bonds, but in the 1930s he began to look at the complex molecules within living things. At first, as Francis Crick and other researchers at the Cavendish Laboratory later did, he studied hemoglobin. He showed in 1949 that sickle-cell anemia, an inherited blood disease, is caused by faulty hemoglobin molecules—the first time an illness was shown to be the result of an abnormal protein. Drawing on knowledge of X-ray crystallography and other physical and chemical data as well as his own technique of model building, Pauling and Robert Corey determined that hemoglobin and most other protein molecules exist in the form of either a helix or a sheet. He announced this discovery in 1951.

Pauling's second Nobel Prize, the Peace Prize for 1962, grew out of his political activism. During the 1950s, he became concerned about the dangers of radioactive contamination from above ground testing of nuclear weapons. He played a major part in the movement that resulted in a 1963 treaty between the United States and the Soviet Union banning such tests.

Reactions to Pauling's ideas covered as wide a range as the theories themselves. Scientists agreed, however, that his proposals were always significant, and he presented them with energy and style. Francis Crick told Horace Judson:

> Pauling [was bold] to the point of rashness. . . . Linus . . . would probably show an idea even if he realized . . . there was a good chance of being wrong. In fact a lot of his ideas *were* wrong. But the ones that were right were important, and therefore he was forgiven.

Linus Pauling died of cancer at his home in Big Sur, California, on August 19, 1994, at the age of 93.

form changed into the other. This paper, to be published in the journal *Acta Crystallographica*, also recounted what she and Gosling had found out about the structure of the DNA molecule, focusing on the fact that the phosphates were on the outside of its intertwined chains. The paper included X-ray photographs of both the A and B forms. A second paper described the results of their Patterson calculations for the A form, and a third summarized the pair's findings on the B form. Franklin still believed at this time that the A form of DNA could not be a helix.

While Franklin was writing her papers, another event took place that would have a major effect on the undeclared "race": Raymond Gosling gave Photo 51, Franklin's exceptionally clear X-ray image of the B form of DNA, to Maurice Wilkins around January 26. Gosling may not have asked Franklin's permission, but he said later that he saw no need to do so. After all, the photo represented his work as much as hers, and it was part of the research on DNA that would continue at the King's laboratory after she had gone. "Maurice had a perfect right to that information," Brenda Maddox quotes him as saying. This photograph, much more than any others that Wilkins had seen (he claimed in his autobiography that Franklin had shown him no pictures of the B form after her November 1951 seminar), convinced him that the B form of DNA *had* to be a helix.

Peter Pauling had asked his father to send a copy of his and Corey's paper on DNA, and the unpublished paper reached the Cavendish on January 28. When Watson read the paper, he saw immediately that Linus Pauling had made a mistake as obvious as the one he and Crick had made in November 1951, which had earned such a contemptuous scolding from Rosalind Franklin. Pauling's proposed model, a three-chain helix with the bases on the outside, was built on an error in basic chemistry; he had forgotten that phosphates in water would carry a positive electrical charge because of the positively charged hydrogen atoms from the water that would be attached to them. Without this charge, Pauling's supposed "nucleic acid" was not an acid at all. Watson also believed that the charge was needed to hold the molecule together.

The *Proceedings of the National Academy of Sciences* was going to publish Pauling's paper in about six weeks. Watson was sure that some other scientist would point out Pauling's mistake as soon as the paper appeared. Pauling would then redo his calculations and, very possibly, find the right answer. Watson therefore felt that he and Crick had only those six weeks as "breathing room" in which to solve the DNA puzzle. They would have to resume their work on the structure immediately, whether anyone else approved of the idea or not.

Rosalind Franklin gave her last seminar at King's on the same day that Watson read Linus Pauling's paper. Her talk focused on the A form of DNA and the reasons why her X-ray photos and calculations led her to believe that this version of the molecule, at least, was not shaped like a helix. She did not mention the B form at all. When Wilkins asked her about it during the question period after her talk, she agreed that the B form was a helix. Wilkins wrote in his autobiography that this was the first time he remembered hearing her say that *any* form of DNA could have a helical shape.

## A STARTLING PHOTO

Two days after Franklin's seminar, Watson visited King's with the Pauling paper in hand. He could not find Wilkins at first, so he strode into Franklin's laboratory and asked whether she wanted to see Pauling's paper. According to Watson's account in *The Double Helix,* she responded only with an irritated glare. He nonetheless launched into an explanation of Pauling's mistakes. Instead of being amused at the similarity between Pauling's model and Watson's own earlier ill-fated effort, Franklin "became increasingly annoyed with my recurring references to helical structures" and informed him that "not a shred of evidence permitted Linus, or anyone else, to postulate a helical structure for DNA." When Watson defended his helix proposal, "her voice rose as she told me that the stupidity of my remarks would be obvious if I would stop blubbering and look at her X-ray evidence."

Irritated himself by now at what he saw as Franklin's blind resistance, and recalling Crick's insistence that her conclusion about the A form was mistaken, Watson replied in kind. "I implied that she was incompetent in interpreting X-ray pictures," he wrote. Franklin, never one to take insults in silence, rounded on the arrogant young man, whom, undoubtedly, she liked no better than he liked her. The startled Watson backed up, fearing, he claimed later, "that in her hot anger she might strike me"—a notion that Franklin supporters such as Anne Sayre have found farfetched, since Franklin was much shorter than Watson.

Watson left Franklin's quarters rapidly. Shortly afterward, he encountered Maurice Wilkins, and they had a long talk about their mutual dislike for Franklin and their relief that she was about to leave King's College. During this conversation, Wilkins showed Franklin's Photo 51 to Watson. Like Gosling before him, Wilkins did not ask Franklin's permission to share her work, but, also like Gosling, he did not feel that he needed to do so. According to Brenda Maddox, Wilkins believed that, as assistant head of the laboratory, he had the right to do as he wished with the products of the lab's research. He also was unaware that Watson and Crick were planning to resume their work on DNA. Wilkins wrote later in his autobiography, "In retrospect, I had been rather foolish to show [the photograph] to Jim. . . . Part of my motive was to justify my exasperation with Rosalind for opposing helical ideas when the evidence seemed to point us clearly in that direction. I had also thought that Jim was already familiar with B patterns."

Photo 51 had not seemed especially important to either Franklin or Wilkins, but its clear indication that the B form of DNA, at least, *had* to be a helix struck Watson like a thunderclap. "The instant I saw the picture my mouth fell open and my pulse began to race," he wrote in *The Double Helix.* Apparently, he had never seen, or at least had not remembered seeing, X-ray photos of the B form before. (It seems likely that Franklin had shown such photos during her November 1951 talk, which Watson attended, since the two forms were the subject of her presentation.)

Watson already knew from William Astbury's photos of DNA that the bases in the DNA molecule were 3.4 A apart, and he and Crick had determined several months before that the diameter of the molecule was 20 A. Wilkins told him that there were 10 nucleotides in a single repeat, or complete turn of the helix, so he quickly calculated that the height of one repeat must be 34 A. He felt that he now had the basic information he needed to begin building a new model. As he rode the train back to Cambridge, he sketched the molecule's probable shape in the margin of his newspaper. By the time he returned to his rooms, he had decided that the DNA helix must have two rather than three chains because, as he wrote in *The Double Helix,* "important biological objects come in pairs."

## BUILDING A NEW MODEL

Lawrence Bragg, the director of the Cavendish Laboratory, shared James Watson's view of Linus Pauling as a rival; Pauling had worked out the basic structure of the protein molecule before Bragg, and the British scientist had never forgotten it. When Bragg learned about Pauling's forthcoming paper, therefore, he gave Watson and Crick permission to resume their work on DNA.

The two men began a new round of model building on February 4. While waiting for the Cambridge machine shop to make metal forms to represent the subunit molecules, Watson spent his days sketching possible models in which the phosphate-sugar backbones were on the inside of the large molecule. He finally admitted that these did not fit the X-ray data, however, and gave in to Crick's insistence that he put the backbones on the outside instead. He quickly saw that this arrangement worked much better—just as Rosalind Franklin had been pointing out for years.

Meanwhile, Maurice Wilkins visited Crick and his wife for lunch. When Crick asked him whether he would mind if Crick and Watson began building models of DNA again, the King's College scientist gave his permission, but he was not happy that what he, too, was beginning to think of as "the DNA Race" was starting up once more. Wilkins wrote in his autobiography:

> I did not like treating science as a race, and I especially did not like the idea of them racing against me. . . . But when I assessed the extent of the logjam in our DNA work at King's, it seemed obvious that I could not ask Francis and Jim to hold off . . . any longer.

Watson, who was also present at the meal, was relieved to hear Wilkins consent, but he admitted in *The Double Helix* that he and Crick would have proceeded even if their rival had refused.

Crick and Watson received a valuable new piece of their puzzle around February 12. Austrian scientist Max Perutz (1914–2002), the head of their laboratory unit, showed them a report that the King's College group had prepared for its funding agency, the Medical Research Council (MRC), in December. The report included a paper by each of the laboratory members, describing the research that he or she had done during the previous year. Perutz had a copy because he was a member of the MRC committee that reviewed the Randall laboratory's performance.

Rosalind Franklin's section of the MRC report contained a piece of information that provided a critical insight for Francis Crick: The A form of DNA, she wrote, existed as "monoclinic C2" crystals. Aaron Klug, who later worked with Franklin, wrote in an article about the discovery of DNA published in Torsten Krude's *DNA: Changing Science and Society* that Franklin had probably mentioned this fact in her November 1951 talk, but Watson had not remembered it because that bit of technical jargon meant nothing to him. Crick, on the other hand, was a trained crystallographer, and by chance he had been studying exactly this kind of crystal in his work on hemoglobin. Any molecule that formed such crystals, he realized, was likely to look the same from either end.

Combined with other facts in Franklin's paper, this information provided strong evidence that the DNA molecule must consist of two helical chains in which the sequences of bases run in opposite directions, like up and down escalators. Franklin herself had missed this implication, although she came close to it by sketching the A form molecule as a figure eight in January 1953. "I could have kicked myself for not noticing it," she later told Aaron Klug, as Klug recounted in Torsten Krude's book.

Like Wilkins's showing of Franklin's DNA photo to Watson, Perutz's passing the MRC report to Watson and Crick without permission from its authors later aroused controversy. In response, Perutz wrote in a letter published in *Science* on June 27, 1969:

> The report was not confidential and contained no data that Watson had not already heard about from Miss Franklin and Wilkins themselves. . . . I realized later that, as a matter of courtesy, I should have asked Randall for permission to show it to Watson and Crick, but in 1953 I was inexperienced and casual in administrative matters and, since the report was not confidential, I saw no reason for withholding it.

Science, like other fields of human activity, has ethical gray areas, and Perutz's action seems to fall into one of these.

## ARRANGING THE BASES

Now that Watson had agreed to put the phosphate-sugar backbones on the outside of their model DNA molecule, he and Crick were left (as Watson wrote in *The Double Helix*) with the "frightful problem . . . of how to pack together two or more chains with irregular sequences of bases." The bases' arrangement was unimportant if they were on the outside of the chains, but if they were inside, it mattered very much—and neither Watson nor Crick had "the slightest ray of light" on what that arrangement might be.

The two men knew that two of the four bases in DNA, *adenine* and *guanine,* belong to a class of biochemicals called *purines* and have similar shapes. *Thymine* and *cytosine,* termed *pyrimidines,* have shapes different from those of adenine and guanine but very much like one another. Crick and Watson were also aware of a discovery about the four bases that Erwin Chargaff (1905–2002), an Austrian refugee scientist working in Britain, had made in 1949 and published in 1950. Chargaff had found that the total amount of purines in a DNA molecule always equals the total amount of pyrimidines. Furthermore, the quantities of adenine and thymine are about the same, and so are the quantities of cytosine and guanine. Chargaff himself had been unable to explain the meaning of these findings. Watson had suspected for some time that Chargaff's discovery would prove important in understanding the way the bases are arranged in the DNA molecule, but he and Crick were not sure how to apply it.

Watson sketched a variety of arrangements, such as pairs of identical bases side-by-side on the two chains, but none of them fitted the dimensions that Franklin's X-ray data specified for the molecule or produced the regular shape that he and Crick were sure it must have. Instead, such patterns made the backbones bulge out in some places and pinch inward in others because of the different sizes and shapes of the bases. This problem was solved only after another new member of the Cambridge group, a crystallographer and physical chemist from the United States named Jerry Donohue (1920–85), provided a final clue.

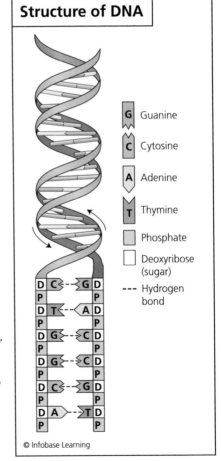

**Structure of DNA**

G Guanine

C Cytosine

A Adenine

T Thymine

▢ Phosphate

▢ Deoxyribose (sugar)

--- Hydrogen bond

James Watson and Francis Crick concluded in 1953 that each molecule of deoxyribonucleic acid (DNA) is made up of two "backbones" composed of alternating smaller molecules of phosphate (P) and deoxyribose (D), a sugar. The backbones both have the shape of a helix, or coil, and they twine around each other. Inside the backbones, like rungs on a twisted ladder, are four kinds of smaller molecules called bases. The bases are in pairs, with the two parts connected by hydrogen bonds. Adenine (A) always pairs with thymine (T), and cytosine (C) always pairs with guanine (G).

© Infobase Learning

Donohue reminded Watson that each of the bases can exist in two forms, called enol and keto, which have slightly different shapes. Watson had assumed that the bases were in the enol form because most biochemistry textbooks showed them that way. Donohue, however, told him that the textbooks were wrong and suggested trying the keto form instead. When Watson followed Donohue's advice, he found that his like-with-like (adenine with adenine, for example) base pairs were not merely awkward but completely impossible because the sizes of the pairs were so different.

Unaware of all this activity at Cambridge, Rosalind Franklin was very busy with her own work. By February 2, she had rejected the idea that the A form of DNA was a figure eight, and she finally turned back to the B form of the molecule on February 10. She alternated between the two forms for the rest of the month. On February 24, she concluded that the A as well as the B form of DNA had the shape of a helix, with two chains of smaller molecules spiraling around one another. She also realized that the two purines were interchangeable in the larger molecule, and so were the two pyrimidines. She did not pass on any of her thoughts to Wilkins, however.

The Cambridge machine shop still had not finished the metal forms of the bases for Watson and Crick's DNA model, so Watson cut shapes out of cardboard and used those for puzzle pieces instead. He had his final revelation about the DNA molecule on Saturday, February 28, when he tried matching adenine with thymine and guanine with cytosine. These pairs—and only these pairs—proved able to form hydrogen bonds with one another and fit inside the sugar-phosphate backbones without distorting the two chains' helical shape. This pairing also perfectly explained Chargaff's ratios. All the parts of the puzzle had come together at last.

## THE MODEL IS FINISHED

Combined with Crick's earlier insight that the order of the bases in the DNA molecule's two chains run in opposite directions, Watson's discovery of the base pairs revealed how DNA could reproduce itself. The hydrogen bonds that (Watson and Crick believed) held the pairs of bases together are weak

---

(*opposite page*) DNA's structure explains its power to duplicate itself. When a cell prepares to divide, the hydrogen bonds between the bases dissolve and the DNA molecule splits along its length like a zipper unzipping. Each half then attracts bases and backbone pieces from among the molecules in the cell, forming the same pairs of bases that had existed before. The result is two identical DNA molecules.

## Replication of DNA

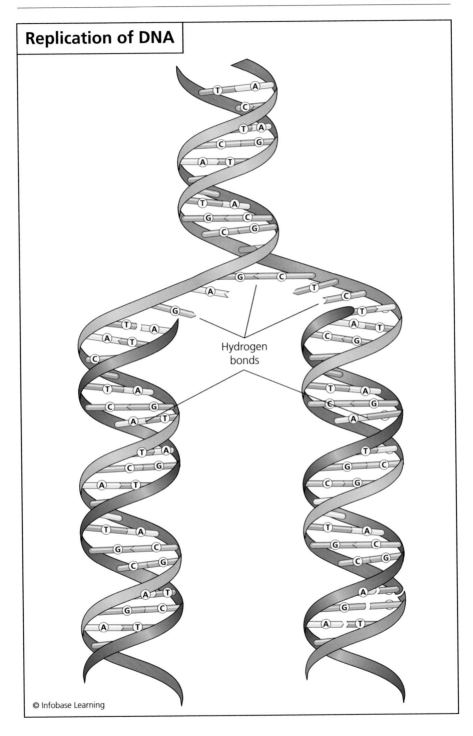

Hydrogen
bonds

and easily broken. If the bonds broke, the molecule could split down the middle. Each base on the two separate chains, which normally twine in parallel around the molecule's axis like the sides of a twisted ladder, could then attract its opposite number, complete with backbone segment (that is, a whole nucleotide), from among the chemicals in the cell. The segments would join together and the hydrogen bonds would re-form, producing two identical pairs of twisted chains from the original one. According to Watson's *Double Helix*, it was after this realization that Crick "winged into the Eagle [the nearby bar] to tell everyone within hearing distance that we had found the secret of life."

"Our dark lady leaves us next week," Maurice Wilkins wrote to Crick on March 7. He was thrilled because Franklin's departure would mean that he could resume his own research on DNA. "At last the decks are clear and we can put all hands to the pumps!" his letter concluded excitedly. "It won't be long now."

Wilkins did not know that it was already too late. Watson and Crick had finally received their metal parts, and, after careful measurements to make sure that all the atoms were placed properly, they completed their model on the same day that Wilkins wrote his letter. The model showed one complete turn of the DNA helix. Although Crick and Watson knew they had not proven that their structure was correct, it fitted all the X-ray data they had, and, as Watson wrote in *The Double Helix*, they were convinced that "a structure this pretty just had to exist."

Crick and Watson invited Wilkins to come to Cambridge and see their model, and he did so on March 12. Wilkins wrote in *The Third Man of the Double Helix:*

> I was rather stunned by it all. . . . A feeling came through to me that the model, though only bits of wire on a lab bench, had a special life of its own. It seemed like an incredible new-born baby that spoke for itself, saying, 'I don't care what you think—I know I am right.'

After Wilkins returned to King's, he wrote to Crick:

> I think you're a couple of old rogues but you may well have something. . . . I might, given a little time, have got it [figured out the DNA molecule's structure]. But there is *no good grousing*—I think it's a very exciting notion & who the hell got it isn't what matters. . . . As one rat to another, good racing.

A jubilant James Watson (left) and Francis Crick are shown here with their final model of the DNA molecule in 1953. The model shows one complete turn of the molecule's double helix. Although the two had little evidence at the time that their proposed structure was correct, they felt sure that, as Watson later put it in his memoir, *The Double Helix*, "a structure this pretty just had to exist." (*A. Barrington Brown/Photo Researchers, Inc.*)

Privately, Wilkins said in his autobiography, he felt a degree of disappointment and anger that he did not express to Crick. Nonetheless, he wrote, "I firmly believed that what really mattered was scientific progress."

## NEAR MISS

Watson and Crick were already drafting a short paper for *Nature* that would describe their proposed structure. A footnote in the paper acknowledged,

"We have . . . been stimulated by a knowledge of the general nature of the unpublished experimental results and ideas of Dr. M. H. F. Wilkins, Dr. R. E. Franklin, and their coworkers at King's College, London." However, Wilkins—and John Randall—insisted on more representation than that.

After discussion with one another and the editors of *Nature,* the groups agreed that three papers would be published together in a single issue of the magazine. The first would be Watson and Crick's paper about the structure of DNA. A paper by Wilkins, Alec Stokes, and Herbert Wilson, offering evidence that DNA in several types of living creatures as well as extracted DNA had a helical form, would appear next. Finally, Franklin and Gosling would describe their work on the B form of DNA—stating that "the structure is probably helical"—in a third paper, which would include the beautiful Photo 51. Franklin had just written such a paper, which she now modified with the sentence, "Thus our general ideas are consistent with the model proposed by Crick and Watson." This sentence turned her original work into a simple piece of supporting research.

Aaron Klug found a draft of this paper dated March 17, before Franklin had heard about the Watson-Crick model, among Franklin's scientific notes (which he inherited after her death). He published an article describing this previously unknown draft in the April 26, 1974, issue of *Nature.* According to Klug, the draft paper showed that at that time, Franklin—who had already moved to Birkbeck—was on the verge of working out the DNA molecule's structure for herself. She recognized that the molecule was a two-chain helix with the phosphate groups on the outside and the bases on the inside. She guessed that cytosine and thymine, the two pyrimidines, were interchangeable, and so were the two purines, adenine and guanine, whereas a purine and a pyrimidine were not. She had not reached the final insights about the one-up-one-down structure of the chains and the specific pairing of the bases, but in a few more months—even weeks or days, perhaps—she might have grasped those facts as well if she had continued to work on DNA.

Klug, Raymond Gosling, and even James Watson have said or written that Franklin might have reached these key insights before Watson and Crick if she had been working with the the right person—someone as compatible with her as Watson and Crick were with one another, or as Klug (whom she did not know at that time) eventually became with her. Klug, for instance, told Horace Freeland Judson, "She needed a collaborator, and she didn't have one. Somebody to break the pattern of her thinking, to show her what was right in front of her, to push her up and over."

Franklin and Gosling followed Wilkins's footsteps to Cambridge a few days after his visit to examine the Watson-Crick model for themselves. When Franklin saw the dimensions that the two Cambridge scientists had used for the molecule, she may have suspected that they had somehow seen her work, since the figures matched her unpublished data. She never complained about it, however. She immediately agreed that their structure was probably right—after all, it fitted with many of her own conclusions—but she felt that they still had to prove its correctness.

By that time, in any case, Rosalind Franklin's mind was no longer on DNA. She merely wanted to finish writing the papers that described her work at King's and turn to new research projects at Birkbeck. To her, DNA was less a "golden molecule" than a reminder of a short, unhappy chapter in her life that she gratefully realized was finally coming to an end.

# Analyzing Viruses

In mid-April 1953, John Randall wrote to Rosalind Franklin at Birkbeck College, ordering her to stop even thinking about DNA as soon as possible—a notion she found ridiculous. She still had several papers to write or modify, describing research on the molecule that was already completed. She also needed to continue working with Raymond Gosling on his Ph.D. thesis, since he had not been given another adviser. She and Gosling therefore went on meeting without Randall's knowledge, and they produced several papers that were published in the spring and summer.

One of these papers, which appeared in *Nature* on July 25, showed that Franklin had finally accepted the idea that the A form as well as the B form of DNA had a helix-shaped molecule with two strands. The Patterson calculations on which she and Gosling had worked so hard provided conclusive crystallographic proof that this was so, the two scientists wrote. In the A form, the bases are tilted by about 25 degrees rather than being perpendicular to the fiber axis as they are in the B form; this tilt is reflected in the fact that A-form fibers are about 30 percent shorter than those of the B form. Franklin and Gosling stated that their results agreed with the Watson-Crick DNA model in principle but not on "points of detail." This paper was the first independent confirmation of Watson and Crick's proposed structure.

## SETTLING IN

Meanwhile, Franklin was trying to settle in at Birkbeck, to which she had transferred on March 1. Physically, the change from King's was like "moving from a palace to the slums," she wrote to Adrienne Weill on March 10. J. D. Bernal's laboratory, her new home, was located in a pair of rickety, bomb-damaged houses originally built in 1835. Franklin's office was on the top floor of one of the houses, but her X-ray equipment was in the basement. The building had no elevator, so she had to climb or descend five flights of stairs in order to move from one to the other.

In spite of this and other annoyances, Franklin found Birkbeck a relatively congenial slum. The laboratory team's politics, for example, were even more liberal than her own; indeed, Bernal had once been a member of the Communist Party and was still an outspoken supporter of the Soviet Union. Franklin wrote to Anne Sayre at the end of 1953 that the group's far-left views sometimes made them narrow-minded. Nonetheless, she felt that they respected her more than her laboratory mates had done at King's College. According to Brenda Maddox, Franklin also found Bernal to be "an understanding and supportive boss."

Rosalind Franklin wrote to a friend that her laboratory at Birkbeck College, shown here in 1958, was "a slum" compared to the one she had had at King's College, but she found her fellow researchers much more congenial. Franklin's office at Birkbeck was on the top floor of a bomb-damaged house, but her X-ray equipment was in the basement, five elevatorless floors below. (*Churchill Archives Centre, Churchill College, Cambridge*)

John Desmond Bernal, shown here, was a pioneer in applying X-ray crystallography to the complex molecules found in living things. He took some of the first X-ray photographs of DNA in the late 1930s. He was head of the laboratory at Birkbeck College in which Rosalind Franklin worked from March 1953 until her death in 1958, and Franklin biographer Brenda Maddox writes that Franklin found him "an understanding and supportive boss." (*Daily Mail/Rex/Alamy*)

Just as had been the case at King's, Franklin spent most of her first year at Birkbeck obtaining and setting up equipment for her research. The X-ray cameras she and Gosling had worked so hard to develop belonged to King's College and remained there, so she had to find new ones. She also read about viruses that cause disease in plants, since one of these, tobacco mosaic virus (TMV for short), was to be her new research subject. This virus shrivels the leaves of tobacco plants and turns parts of the leaves from their normal green to a sickly white, producing a mottled or mosaic pattern.

Viruses have features in common with both living and nonliving things. Outside of living cells, they are inert combinations of protein and nucleic acid (DNA or RNA). They can even form crystals much like those of inorganic compounds. When a virus touches a cell, however, it becomes active, injecting its nucleic acid into the cell like a microscopic hypodermic needle. The nucleic acid takes over the cell's genetic machinery and forces it to copy the virus's genes instead of its own. These genetic particles then break out of the cell, acquiring protein coats and destroying the cell in the process. They become new viruses that go on to infect other cells. In this way, viruses reproduce.

Tobacco mosaic virus causes a disease in tobacco plants that make the plant's leaves shrink and become mottled with patches of sickly white. The tobacco plant on the left is healthy, but the plant on the right has been infected with tobacco mosaic disease. *(Grant Heilman Photography/Alamy)*

## How Viruses Reproduce

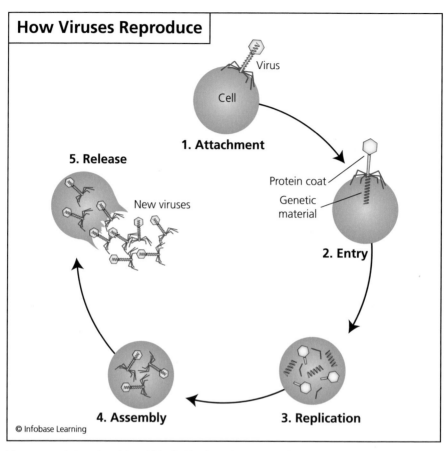

Virus

Cell

**1. Attachment**

**5. Release**

Protein coat

New viruses

Genetic material

**2. Entry**

**4. Assembly**

**3. Replication**

© Infobase Learning

Viruses, consisting of nucleic acid (coiled line) inside a protein shell, can reproduce only inside living cells. A virus first attaches itself to a cell by locking onto a receptor molecule on the cell's surface (1). It then injects its genetic material (DNA or RNA) into the cell like a miniature hypodermic needle, leaving its protein covering outside (2). This material takes over the cell's gene-copying machinery and forces it to make copies of the virus's genes instead (3). The copies are covered with new protein capsules (4). Finally, the completed viruses break out of the cell, destroying it in the process, and go on to infect other cells (5).

In 1952, while Watson and Crick were forced to stop working on DNA, James Watson had turned his attention to TMV and found evidence that its subunits form a helix. He thought that the virus's nucleic acid, RNA, was a central core inside this spiral of protein molecules, like a wick in a candle. Having learned quite a bit of crystallography from Crick by that time, Watson took X-ray pictures of TMV in June that seemed to support his proposal. Both building on and testing Watson's work, Franklin hoped to discover the details of TMV's inner structure. By the end of 1953, she was

# TOBACCO MOSAIC VIRUS: THE FIRST KNOWN VIRUS

Tobacco mosaic virus was the first virus to be identified. Martinus Bei-jerinck (1851–1931), a Dutch botanist and microbiologist, described it in 1898. He showed that liquid squeezed from infected plants could produce tobacco mosaic disease when injected into other plants, even after it was strained through a filter with pores tiny enough to stop the passage of bacteria, the smallest living things then known. This meant that whatever caused the disease must be even more minute than bacteria. Beijerinck called the "contagious living fluid" that transmitted the disease a virus, from the Latin word for "poison." Neither he nor other researchers who later named viruses as the likely cause of other diseases had any idea what these microorganisms really were. No one could see viruses until electron microscopes were invented in the 1930s.

Most early virus studies were done on TMV because it was simple, stable, and highly infectious. Huge quantities of the virus could be grown

*(continued)*

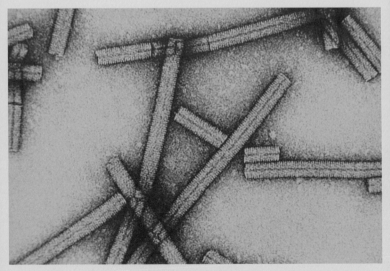

This electron micrograph shows tobacco mosaic virus magnified 500,000 times. This virus was the first to be discovered and the first to be studied extensively. *(Peter Arnold, Inc./Alamy)*

*(continued)*

easily from just a few tobacco plants, and it could be handled safely because it did not harm humans or animals. TMV was the first virus to be purified and the first to be photographed by X-rays. Wendell Stanley (1904–71), a virologist at the University of California, Berkeley, showed that it could form crystals in 1935, and J. D. Bernal and Isidor Fankuchen (1904–64), a crystallographer from the United States, used X-ray crystallography in 1941 to provide evidence that the virus appeared to be made up of identical "submolecules" of protein. They did not know how these subunits were arranged, however, or where the RNA that the virus was also found to contain was located. Rosalind Franklin hoped to solve these mysteries.

producing beautiful X-ray photographs of TMV. She applied Patterson calculations to these photographs in early 1954.

## FIRST VISIT TO THE UNITED STATES

In early 1954, Rosalind Franklin was pleased to receive an invitation to speak at the Gordon Research Conference, a highly regarded series of meetings that the American Association for the Advancement of Science held each summer in New Hampshire. The conference, which was on a different subject every year, featured coal and related substances that year. The conference organizers were therefore asking Franklin to talk about her original area of expertise.

Franklin had mixed feelings about the United States. She held some common British prejudices against "loud" Americans, but she had never seen the country itself, and, as always, she was curious about other lands and cultures. She also hoped to visit several laboratories in the United States where exciting work in her new field, *virology* (the study of viruses), was being done.

Raising enough money for the trip was not easy, however. The organizers of the Gordon Conference did not provide funds for overseas travel, and the new sponsor of Franklin's research, the British government's Agricultural Research Council (ARC), refused to pay anything toward the project.

Only with difficulty did Franklin piece together enough small grants to pay for her journey, usually by promising to speak about either coal or viruses at various universities.

During Franklin's journey to the United States, which lasted from about August through October 1954, she was an eager tourist and wrote long letters about her experience to her parents. Brenda Maddox quotes some of these in her Franklin biography. "The overwhelming impression so far is of overabundance of everything and the resulting complete self-confidence of individuals," Franklin wrote soon after her arrival, for instance. Her most exciting adventure was living through a hurricane during a visit to the Marine Biological Laboratory at Woods Hole, on the Cape Cod peninsula of Massachusetts, a little south of Boston.

In the part of her travels related to science, Franklin wrote, she met two "very different" groups of people. One was the coal industrialists and researchers, who were "quite pleasant" and respectful to her because of the work she had done in Paris "but not very interesting." The second group, the virus scientists and other investigators in fundamental biology, were much less aware of her reputation for the most part but had "first-class" minds— the highest compliment in Rosalind Franklin's vocabulary.

Among the researchers Franklin visited during her U.S. trip was James Watson, whom she saw at Woods Hole and later at Linus Pauling's home university, Caltech, in Pasadena, California. Strange as it might seem considering their former ill feelings, Franklin had become friends with both Watson and Crick in the years after the discovery of the DNA double helix. She had grown especially close to Crick and his wife, Odile. She saw less of Watson, who had returned to the United States soon after the DNA discovery, but they kept in touch because both of them were working on viruses that contained RNA. At Caltech, Franklin also finally met Linus Pauling, the third contestant in the great "race" that she had never acknowledged participating in.

By the end of her journey to the United States, Franklin had obtained many new contacts, virus samples, and promises of cooperation in future research. She had also developed a new attitude toward the country and its people. "For Rosalind," Brenda Maddox writes, "Americans now fell into the category of foreigners with whom she felt at home."

## BUILDING A RESEARCH TEAM

Franklin was beginning to find people in the Birkbeck laboratory with whom she felt at home as well. Her most important coworker was Aaron

Klug, a chemist, theoretical physicist, and crystallographer from South Africa whom she met in 1954 when he moved into the other office on the laboratory building's fifth floor. At first, Klug was working on a different project, but when she showed him some of the photographs she had made of tobacco mosaic virus, he became fascinated and asked to join her research. "It was Rosalind Franklin who set me the example of tackling large and difficult problems," Klug said in the lecture he gave in Sweden after receiving the Nobel Prize in chemistry in 1982 for his work on virus structure.

Klug was Franklin's equal in talent; they also had their Jewish background in common. Brenda Maddox wrote that he "shared and sharpened [Franklin's] ideas, . . . could argue with her and share the day-to-day excite-

Sir Aaron Klug, shown here in 1992, met Rosalind Franklin in 1954 and became her closest collaborator. Together they made important discoveries about the structure of tobacco mosaic virus and other plant viruses. Klug won the Nobel Prize in chemistry in 1982 for his work on the structure of viruses, which continued after Franklin's death. (*John Cole/Photo Researchers, Inc.*)

ment and discovery" of the virus work—in other words, he was exactly the kind of collaborator she had needed so badly during her DNA research. Franklin and Klug seem to have understood one another completely, even though in some ways they were very different. Unlike the intensely logical Franklin, for instance, Klug was (according to writer Dan Jacobson, a close friend of Klug's, who is quoted by Brenda Maddox) "imaginative and playful and artistic." His deductive approach to science and life helped to balance her inductive one.

A far less pleasant relationship developed between Franklin and Norman Pirie (1907–97), an eminent British biochemist. Early in 1955, Franklin wrote several papers describing her research on TMV and sent one to Pirie for comment. Pirie was such an expert on plant viruses that he felt he "owned" the field, and he became very angry when anyone—especially a younger person or a woman—challenged his findings. Unfortunately for Franklin, who was both of those things, her paper did exactly that. Pirie had claimed that TMV particles had different lengths, but Franklin said her X-ray photos showed that they were all rods or cylinders 3,000 angstroms long. She claimed that the protein subunits making up each virus were all the same size as well.

Pirie sent Franklin a condescending, disrespectful letter telling her in no uncertain terms that she was wrong. She politely defended her work—and correctly so, as later research would show. Right or wrong, however, she knew that Pirie's anger was dangerous. His laboratory grew a variety of plant viruses, and he had supplied her with useful ones in the past. He now refused to do so any longer, so she knew she would have to find other sources or culture the viruses herself. Worse still, Pirie was a close friend of Sir William Slater, the secretary of the Agricultural Research Council, which funded Franklin's research. Pirie could, and did, make sure she had to fight for every piece of equipment or salary grant that she requested.

By this time, Franklin and Klug were expanding their studies beyond TMV. They wanted to compare TMV's structure to those of several other viruses that cause plant diseases, such as the turnip yellow mosaic virus and the tomato bushy stunt virus. Their requests to other scientists eventually brought them samples of such viruses from all over the world.

Some of these plant viruses had cylindrical shapes like TMV, while others were spherical. Franklin and Klug agreed that she would continue to study TMV and other rod-shaped viruses, while he would explore the round ones. They hoped to learn how protein and nucleic acid units were arranged in each of the viruses.

To carry out this broader work, Franklin and Klug needed to increase the size of their laboratory staff. Through classified advertisements placed in *Nature* they acquired two assistants, Ph.D. students Kenneth Holmes and John Finch, during the first half of 1955. Finch came from Franklin's old nemesis, King's College, while Holmes was from St. John's College, part of Cambridge University. The group decided that Holmes would assist Franklin, while Finch worked with Klug. The National Coal Board paid a third assistant, graduate student James Watt, to help Franklin continue her research on coal.

The fourth and final new team member was a young biophysicist from Yale University named Don Caspar. Unlike the other three, Caspar had already earned his Ph.D. He had even made a major discovery: While still at Yale, he had shown that the tobacco mosaic virus was a hollow cylinder of protein whose center was filled, not with the virus's RNA as most virologists had expected, but with water. This meant that the location of the RNA still needed to be determined. Unknown to Caspar, Rosalind Franklin was obtaining similar results at about the same time.

Caspar first heard about Franklin from James Watson, with whom he had worked on TMV at Caltech during Caspar's postdoctoral period. Caspar wrote to her in April 1955, asking to join her group after he had completed some additional research at Cambridge. Franklin said he would be welcome, and he arrived in early September. He stayed in England for only about a year, but he and Franklin remained close friends after he returned to the United States.

## MONEY WORRIES AND RESEARCH ADVANCES

Franklin came to think of the plant virus research team as her family. She felt very protective of them and argued constantly with the ARC about their salaries as well as her own. Since she did not teach, she had no academic standing at the University of London, and she had both lower pay and less job security than a professor would have had. As she explained in a letter to J. D. Bernal in mid-1955 (quoted in Brenda Maddox's book), written after the ARC had refused to give her a raise:

> My present salary is less than I should be receiving if I had made a career either in university teaching or in the Scientific Civil Service, and is also less than the *average* received by physicists of my age. In view of the fact that I have no security of employment, and nevertheless hold a position of considerable responsibility, this seems to me entirely unjust.

Bernal agreed with Franklin, but he had no power over the ARC.

Franklin herself had a stormy interview with Sir William Slater in September, but she failed to gain any of her requests. She suspected that Slater's own prejudice against women was combining with Pirie's disapproving influence to block her at every turn. She told Anne Sayre that she believed the ARC had denied her requests "because the ARC refuses to support any project that has a woman directing it."

In spite of the financial threats hanging over them, Franklin and her new team produced exciting research in the mid-1950s. Anne Sayre's book notes that Franklin authored 17 papers on virus structure, alone or with other team members, between 1953 and 1958. "Moreover, all this was pioneering work . . . and it was immensely complex work, far more testing, in a technical sense, than [Franklin's] DNA work. . . . [It] represented a giant step taken in something close to the dark." Their studies shed new light on the way proteins and nucleic acids interact in living things and seemed likely to reveal important information about viruses that infect animals and humans as well as those that attack plants.

To begin with, the paper that had caused so much dispute with Pirie, which was published in 1955, also stated that Franklin's data confirmed "most satisfactorily" James Watson's conclusion that the protein subunits in TMV are arranged in a helical pattern, although her opinion differed from Watson's about how many subunits exist in each turn of the helix. The Franklin team's calculations of the distribution of density along the virus's radius suggested for the first time that TMV's RNA might be buried among its subunits rather than running down the center of the virus.

A little later, Franklin's group used a new technique called *heavy-atom isomorphous replacement,* in which a few atoms of a heavy element such as mercury or lead are substituted for atoms in a virus or other large molecule. Comparing the X-ray patterns of the original and altered molecules showed the molecules' structure more clearly than had ever been possible before. Franklin and Don Caspar were among the first to apply this technique to materials that do not form crystals. With it, they showed in 1956 that TMV's RNA coils like a snake among the subunits that make up the virus's hollow cylinder, completely hidden inside this lumpy protein sheath. Franklin confirmed this conclusion by comparing X-ray maps of the normal TMV molecule with maps of TMV particles from which the nucleic acid had been removed. The RNA, she concluded, lies about 40 A from the center of the virus. In one of her papers she speculated that the virus's RNA, unlike the

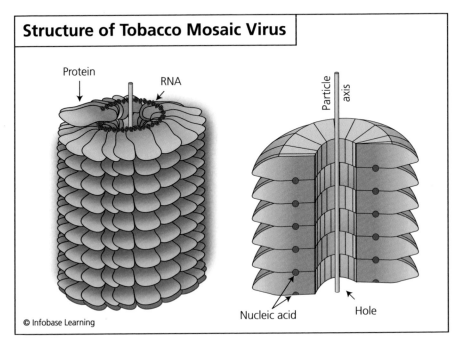

## Structure of Tobacco Mosaic Virus

Protein

RNA

Particle axis

Nucleic acid

Hole

© Infobase Learning

Rosalind Franklin and her research team worked out the structure of tobacco mosaic virus in the mid-1950s. They found that the virus has the shape of a lumpy cylinder, made up of identical protein subunits coiled in a helix shape. The center of the virus is hollow. The RNA that composes the virus's genetic material is coiled like a snake among the protein subunits.

DNA in cell nuclei, possesses only a single strand or chain. This guess was later shown to be correct.

## GOOD NEWS, BAD NEWS

The organizers of the Gordon Conference again invited Franklin to speak there in 1956. That year's subject was nucleic acids, so she could talk about her current work. The chance to see the United States again lifted her spirits, as did the fact that her friend Don Caspar would be attending the conference. She did not have to worry about travel money this time, since the Rockefeller Foundation had offered to pay all her expenses. Her grant included enough money for her to make another tour of American virology laboratories as well.

Franklin enjoyed her return to the United States, since the country was more familiar to her this time. She already knew many of the scientists she saw at the conference and on her travels, which took her to many of the same places she had visited before. She especially enjoyed spending time with Don

Caspar. Both single, the two were beginning to become more than simply compatible coworkers. Brenda Maddox believes that in time their relationship might have ripened into marriage.

Franklin's happiness seemed complete when news of another honor reached her during her stay at the Gordon Conference in New Hampshire. Sir Lawrence Bragg, on behalf of the Royal Institution of London, asked her to make large models of cylindrical and spherical viruses for a science exhibit to be shown at the upcoming World's Fair, which would be held in Brussels, Belgium, in April 1957. These models would make her group's discoveries known throughout the world.

Unfortunately, Franklin never had the chance to present her models. While still in the United States, she experienced bouts of abdominal pain severe enough to warrant a visit to a doctor. He gave her pain medication and recommended that she speak to her personal physician upon her return home. Just before she left the United States in late August, she also noticed that she was having trouble zipping her skirts. She was not gaining weight, yet her abdomen was bulging.

When Franklin returned to London, she described her symptoms to the University College Hospital doctor. After an examination, he sent her to a

Rosalind Franklin is shown here during her second trip to the United States, made in 1956. During this visit, she spoke about her research at a major scientific conference and visited several virology laboratories. Abdominal pains that she suffered toward the end of the trip were the first signs of the ovarian cancer that caused her death a year and a half later. (*Churchill Archives Centre, Churchill College, Cambridge*)

surgeon, who felt a large mass in the left side of her abdomen. The surgeon asked her to check herself into the hospital for an exploratory operation. This surgery, performed on September 4, 1956, revealed two tumors on her ovaries, one the size of a tennis ball and the other even larger. The larger one was cancerous, so the surgeon decided to remove both ovaries.

Franklin felt much better after the operation, which both she and the surgeon believed had removed all the cancer. Impatient with illness as she had always been, she returned to work as soon as she could. She did not tell her laboratory team what had been wrong with her. Cancer was rarely discussed in those days, and Franklin was a very private person who seldom talked about her troubles.

## STRUGGLING IN NEW DIRECTIONS

Money problems were again looming for Franklin's team, thanks partly to the continuing opposition of Norman Pirie and Sir William Slater. Slater had warned Franklin that the ARC was likely to end its funding for her group in April 1957. Unable to find any other support in Britain, Franklin applied for a grant from the U.S. National Institutes of Health (NIH), pointing out that her team's work on plant viruses seemed likely to cast light on RNA-containing viruses that cause human disease.

In early 1957, Franklin continued her work on plant viruses and on preparing the five-foot- [1.5-m]-high virus models for the Brussels World's Fair. Her group was investigating, among other things, similarities between spherical RNA plant viruses and RNA-containing bodies in cells now called *ribosomes,* which help the cell make proteins; Caspar, Crick, and Watson, among others, were also pursuing this connection. Franklin's team showed that the structure of RNA in ribosomes and viruses was quite different from that of isolated RNA because the RNA was embedded in protein in both of these living structures.

Franklin came into the laboratory every day, but she found she had energy for only half-days of work. Even that ended abruptly in April, when episodes of pain and bleeding sent her to the hospital several times. Surgery revealed that a new tumor was growing in her abdomen. She began a course of radiation treatments in the hope of slowing the cancer's growth, though her doctors warned her that a complete cure was unlikely.

The treatments made Franklin feel well enough to attend and sometimes even speak at scientific meetings during the summer, as well take several trips to continental Europe to spend time with family and old friends. She also received good news about her laboratory's funding. She had learned in April

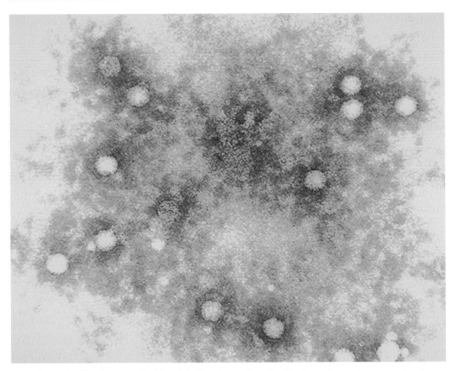

Near the end of her life, Rosalind Franklin began studies of poliovirus, shown here magnified about 46,000 times. She was not allowed to do this research at Birkbeck because the virus causes a serious disease that was greatly feared at the time. *(PHOTOTAKE Inc./Alamy)*

that, thanks to Bernal's appeal to the ARC chairman, Lord Rothschild, the group's ARC grant would be renewed for one more year in spite of Slater's opposition. She found out in early July that they had been awarded a generous sum from the NIH as well. This grant would cover three full years of work.

Franklin even began a new area of research that summer, on the virus that causes *poliomyelitis (polio)*. Polio, a highly contagious disease, was common at the time, especially among children, and can cause permanent paralysis or death. Franklin wanted to study the poliovirus because it seemed similar to the turnip yellow mosaic virus, which her group had already examined.

In the mid-1950s, fear concerning polio was rampant. Jonas Salk (1914–95), a virologist in the United States, had created a vaccine against the disease in 1955, but many still questioned the vaccine's effectiveness. The dirty, rundown buildings that housed Franklin's laboratory had no security features to contain dangerous microorganisms, and the staff at Birkbeck was afraid that the deadly virus might escape and infect people. They insisted, therefore, that Franklin not be allowed to store poliovirus or conduct research on it there. Franklin and Bernal downplayed the danger, but the staff won the argument.

Franklin finally was allowed to store her virus at the nearby London School of Hygiene and Tropical Medicine and X-ray it at the Royal Institution. She did not live long enough to do significant work on poliovirus, but Finch and Klug confirmed in 1959 that the virus has a structure very similar to that of the spherical plant viruses they had studied earlier.

## DEATH COMES TOO SOON

Franklin's abdominal tumor began growing vigorously again in November 1957. She checked into the Royal Marsden Hospital, which specialized in cancer treatment—a fact that told her research team for the first time what her illness was. There she received chemotherapy, which was just starting to be used against cancer. Although she hoped the drug therapy would slow the tumor's growth, Franklin accepted that her illness was probably fatal. In the last months of 1957, she alternated between the hospital, her own apartment, and the homes of family members, especially her brother Roland and his wife. She named all three brothers as executors of the will she made in December. She left the bulk of her money to Aaron Klug, whose family, she knew, needed the extra support.

By early January 1958, Franklin felt well enough to leave the hospital and return to the laboratory part time, though she continued to have treatments as an outpatient. She could not do much research because of problems in obtaining some of the materials she needed, but this frustration was offset by several pieces of good news. First, in February, Birkbeck finally gave her an academic appointment and title, research associate in biophysics. More important, Max Perutz invited her and Klug to move to Cambridge, where he was building a new laboratory, when their NIH grant ended. This invitation, Franklin knew, essentially guaranteed that her team's work would continue, no matter what happened to her.

Franklin was working full days in the laboratory by the end of March, finishing research on plant viruses that she hoped to present at a scientific conference in August. This effort left her so exhausted that she could barely climb the five flights of stairs from her X-ray equipment to her office. Her assistants offered to carry her, but she refused.

Although Franklin continued to hope that her illness could be cured, it was clear to everyone around her that nothing could stop the rapidly advancing cancer. She died in the hospital on April 16, 1958, and was buried in the Franklin family plot at the United Jewish Cemetery in Willesden, a district of London. Her epitaph read, "Scientist: her work on viruses was of lasting benefit to mankind."

Obituary notices, mostly stressing Franklin's work on viruses, appeared in national newspapers and major science journals. For instance, J. D. Bernal wrote in *Nature* on July 19, 1958, "As a scientist Miss Franklin was distinguished by extreme clarity and perfection in everything she undertook. Her photographs are among the most beautiful X-ray photographs of any substance ever taken."

Rosalind Franklin was only 37 years old when she died. As Brenda Maddox has written, Watson and Crick might have deprived Franklin of some of the credit she deserved for her part in solving the structure of the DNA molecule, but the cancer cheated her of something far more important: her life, and with it, all the research achievements she might have given to the world.

# 7

# The Golden Molecule

James Watson's sister Elizabeth, who was visiting him in England, typed the short paper in which he and Crick announced their proposed structure for the DNA molecule. According to Watson's memoir, *The Double Helix,* Watson told her that she "was participating in perhaps the most famous event in biology since [Charles] Darwin's book [*On the Origin of Species,* published in 1859]."

"A Structure for Deoxyribose Nucleic Acid" was published in the April 25, 1953, issue of *Nature.* It was a very short paper—little more than 900 words—that began "We wish to suggest a structure for the salt of deoxyribose nucleic acid. This structure has novel features that are of considerable biological interest." Almost 50 years later, in celebration of the almost-finished decoding of the human *genome* (complete collection of genetic material) at the White House in 2000, President Bill Clinton called the paper's second sentence "one of the greatest understatements of all time" because the "novel features" of DNA's structure that Watson and Crick referred to so casually in fact underlay the decoding of the human genome and most other research on genes that had taken place since the publication of their landmark paper. The paper's final sentence, "It has not escaped our notice that the specific pairing we have postulated immediately suggests a possible copying mechanism for the genetic material," became equally famous.

Watson and Crick spelled out the meaning of their discovery more explicitly in a longer paper, "Genetical Implications of the Structure of

Deoxyribonucleic Acid," which appeared in *Nature* on May 30, 1953, and in "The Complementary Structure of Deoxyribonucleic Acid," published in the *Proceedings of the Royal Society* in 1954. In these papers, the two scientists described how they thought the DNA molecule's structure allowed it to encode genetic information and reproduce itself. By this time, they were confident that their proposed structure was right because they had seen that it agreed with the data that Rosalind Franklin, Raymond Gosling, and Maurice Wilkins had published in the papers accompanying their first one in *Nature*.

## A QUESTION OF CREDIT

Scientists constantly build on one another's work, but when they do so, it is customary for them to credit those other scientists by name and cite the specific papers they have used. Anne Sayre, Brenda Maddox, and a number of other writers have criticized Watson and Crick for giving little explicit credit to Rosalind Franklin for her X-ray work, which directly contributed to their ideas about DNA's structure. In their first paper, they said only, referring to the papers by Franklin and Wilkins in the same issue of the magazine, "We were not aware of the details of the results presented there when we devised our structure, which rests mainly though not entirely on published experimental data and stereochemical arguments." This was technically true, but it glossed over the real state of affairs: Watson and Crick had not seen Franklin and Wilkins's papers, but thanks to Watson's conversations with Wilkins, they had known about most of the research data that the papers contained. Similarly, near the end of the 1954 *Royal Society* paper, Watson and Crick wrote, "We are most indebted to Dr. M. H. F. Wilkins both for informing us of unpublished experimental observations and for the benefit of numerous discussions"—without mentioning that the observations were not Wilkins's own, but rather were Rosalind Franklin's.

Both Sayre and Maddox found this lack of credit more blameworthy than Watson and Crick's obtaining and use of Franklin's data. Sayre, for instance, wrote in her biography of Franklin that the two Cambridge scientists could either have limited discussion in their first paper to DNA's pairing of bases—a very important discovery that they unquestionably made—or else offered Franklin joint authorship of a paper describing the molecule's structure as a whole. As it was, Sayre felt that "the glory was hogged."

Maddox and Sayre also criticized Watson and Crick for never telling Franklin directly that they had seen her unpublished material and gained key facts about the DNA structure from it, even in later years when she had become more friendly with them. As a result, Franklin apparently never knew that this breach of her scientific privacy had occurred. To be sure, such an admission would have taken courage. If Franklin had known the truth, Anne Sayre speculated, "Rosalind might well have risen like a goddess in her wrath, and . . . the thunderbolts might have been memorable."

## MIXED RECEPTION

A few people, including Watson and Crick's supposed chief rival, Linus Pauling, immediately recognized their discovery of the DNA molecule's structure for the groundbreaking achievement it was. Pauling saw their model on a stopover in England on the way to a scientific conference in Belgium near the beginning of April 1953. Robert Olby's history of the DNA discovery, *The Path to the Double Helix,* quotes him as saying during the conference, "I think that the formulation of their [DNA] structure by Watson and Crick may turn out to be the greatest development in the field of molecular genetics in recent years."

Watson also attracted considerable attention when he presented the model during a conference at Cold Spring Harbor Laboratories, in Long Island, New York, in summer 1953. François Jacob (1920–  ) of the Institut Pasteur (quoted in Victor K. McElheny's biography of Watson, *Watson and DNA*) said later that Watson's speech had been the "star turn" of the symposium. Jacob had been unimpressed by Watson and Crick's original paper because he did not understand their crystallographic arguments, but he shared the audience's stunned reaction to Watson's Cold Spring Harbor talk:

> For a moment [after the end of Watson's presentation], the room remained silent. There were a few questions. . . . But no criticism. No objections. This structure was of such simplicity, such perfection, such harmony, such beauty even, and biological advantages flowed from it with such rigor and clarity, that one could not believe it to be untrue.

Many scientists viewed the discovery with less excitement, however. After all, Linus Pauling had just published a proposed DNA structure, but it was discredited almost immediately with basic knowledge of chemistry; why should these two unknowns have anything more substantial to say? Most biochemists still believed that the genetic material would prove to be protein,

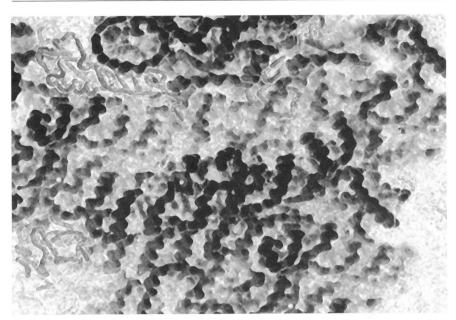

Watson and Crick's discovery of the structure of DNA, to which Rosalind Franklin contributed so much, launched new lines of research that still continue. This picture is a scanning electron micrograph of the two types of nucleic molecule, showing DNA in blue and RNA in red. *(PHOTOTAKE Inc./Alamy)*

so they saw little reason to care about the structure of DNA. Maurice Wilkins wrote in *The Third Man of the Double Helix*, "Many scientists, strange though it may seem now, were too set in their ways to recognize the importance of the model." Watson and Crick's proposed structure for DNA encountered a "lukewarm reception" throughout the 1950s, Robert Olby claimed in "Quiet Debut for the Double Helix," an article that appeared in the January 23, 2003, issue of *Nature*.

Even those researchers who recognized the potential importance of Watson and Crick's discovery wanted to see proof that the model was correct before they accepted it. Maurice Wilkins became a leader in gathering such proof. During the remainder of the 1950s, while Rosalind Franklin was studying plant viruses at Birkbeck, Wilkins continued DNA research at King's College and took excellent X-ray photographs (ultimately far better than Franklin's, thanks to improved technology) that supported and refined Watson and Crick's proposed structure. He and the other King's researchers also showed that the B form of DNA was the natural one, found in species ranging from bacteria to humans.

# FROM GENES TO PROTEINS

Long before DNA was identified as the key substance of which genes are made, scientists realized that the genetic material has to be able to do two things. The first is to reproduce itself, so that when a cell divides, each of the two offspring cells can receive a complete copy of the original cell's genetic information. Watson and Crick's second paper in *Nature* described how this might be accomplished, and two Caltech researchers, Matthew Meselson and Franklin Stahl, published a key experiment in 1958 that proved the correctness of their proposal.

The second major task that genetic material must accomplish is to express itself—put the information it carries into action—by making proteins, the workhorses of the cell. (George Beadle [1903–89] and Edward Tatum [1909–75] had shown in 1941 that a single gene carries the instructions for making a single protein. Researchers learned later that some genes do different kinds of work, such as turning other genes on or off, but making proteins remains the job of most genes.) During the 1950s, Francis Crick turned his attention to finding out how DNA stores the instructions for making proteins and how it translates those instructions into finished protein molecules.

Crick was thinking about the first part of this subject while he and Watson were still preparing their landmark papers on DNA. The two scientists knew that the four bases could appear in any order, or sequence, along the length of a single strand of the DNA helix; the base-pairing rule then determined the sequence in the second strand. Crick believed that genetic information must somehow be represented in the sequence of bases, though the idea was just an unproven proposal, or *hypothesis,* at that time. In March 1953, he wrote to his son, Michael:

> We think we have found the basic mechanism by which life comes from life. . . . It is like a code. If you are given one set of letters you can write down the others. . . . The order of the bases [in DNA] (the letters) makes one gene different from another gene (just as one page of print is different from another).

When thinking about the DNA "code," Crick at first encountered the same stumbling block that had kept most scientists from believing Oswald Avery's results in the late 1940s: How could DNA, with only four kinds of bases, contain the instructions for making proteins, which are combinations of 20 different kinds of amino acids? No protein contains all 20 types of these smaller molecules, but genes had to have a "code letter" for each of the 20 in order to make all the kinds of proteins.

Strangely enough, the first clue to this riddle's answer came, not from a geneticist, but from a physicist and cosmologist (scientist who studies the origin and evolution of the universe) in the United States, George Gamow (1904–68). In a letter that Gamow wrote to Crick in late 1953 after seeing Crick and Watson's articles in *Nature,* Gamow suggested that each "word" of the code might consist of a sequence of three bases. A total of 64 such sequences ($4 \times 4 \times 4$) was possible, which would be more than enough to provide a different sequence for each amino acid.

Crick thought that some of Gamow's ideas about the way the genetic code worked were "bizarre," but he decided that the basic concept was correct. He and South African scientist Sydney Brenner (1927–   ), with whom Crick worked at Cambridge for 20 years beginning in 1957, developed their own version of the three-base code idea in the late 1950s. Then, during the 1960s, a number of researchers, especially a team led by Marshall Nirenberg (1927–   ), a young biochemist at the National Institutes of Health in the United States, worked out the DNA code word by word—that is, they determined which amino acid each possible group of three bases represents.

George Gamow proposed that DNA forms proteins directly, but both Francis Crick and James Watson knew that this idea had to be wrong. DNA normally does not leave the cell nucleus and proteins were known to be made in the *cytoplasm,* the main substance of the cell in which the nucleus is embedded. Some other molecule therefore had to carry DNA's message out to the cytoplasm. The most likely candidate was DNA's chemical cousin, RNA. Both Crick and Watson turned their attention to RNA in the late 1950s, but they no longer worked together; Watson returned to the United States in September 1953 and spent the rest of his career there.

While Watson studied the structure of RNA, Crick, with Brenner's help, focused on the process by which this second nucleic acid helps DNA make proteins. First, Crick and Brenner concluded, DNA copies its code sequence into a molecule of RNA, in which a base named *uracil* is substituted for DNA's thymine. This RNA, later called *messenger RNA,* travels through the wall of the nucleus into the cytoplasm. There it attracts what Crick called "adaptor molecules"—later identified as a second form of RNA, termed *transfer RNA.* Each molecule of transfer RNA contains just three bases, a single "word" in the genetic code, and attaches itself to a molecule of the amino acid represented by that word. The transfer RNA molecules then line up along the longer messenger RNA molecule in an order determined by the messenger RNA, hauling their amino acid cargoes with them like tugboats pulling ships into a row of docks. With the help of ribosomes, the amino acids then attach to one another, forming a protein. Crick, Brenner, and many other researchers spent the late 1950s and 1960s working out this process, the details of which proved to be immensely complex.

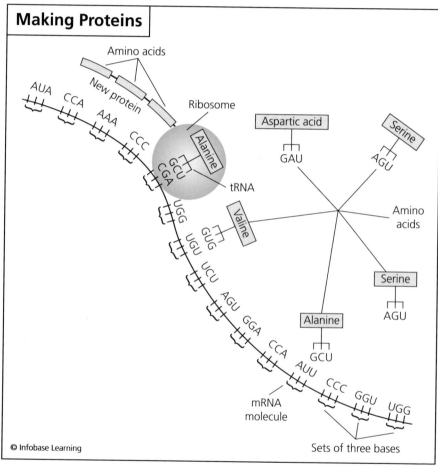

**Making Proteins**

© Infobase Learning

As a first step in making a protein, part of a DNA molecule (a gene) uses itself as a pattern to form a matching stretch of messenger RNA (mRNA). When the messenger RNA moves into the cytoplasm of the cell, it attracts matching short stretches of transfer RNA (tRNA), each of which tows a single amino acid molecule. With the help of a small body called a ribosome, the transfer RNA molecules lock onto the matching parts of the messenger RNA, and the amino acids they carry are joined, forming a protein.

## THE ULTIMATE PRIZE

In 1962, James Watson, Francis Crick, and Maurice Wilkins shared the ultimate scientific award: the Nobel Prize. They received that year's prize in physiology or medicine for their work on DNA. As part of the award ceremonies, each gave a lecture describing the work for which he had won the prize. In these long lectures, Wilkins mentioned Rosalind Franklin only once and Watson and Crick did not refer to her at all. In fairness, it should be said that Watson and Crick's lectures (and most of Wilkins's) did not deal with the discovery of DNA's structure, but rather with later work on these nucleic acids, in which Franklin took no part. Watson did briefly discuss RNA-containing plant viruses, however, and he could have cited Franklin's work at Birkbeck in this context.

There was no question of including Franklin in the award, because Nobel Prizes are never given after someone's death. A number of writers at the time and since, however, have debated about whether she would—or at least should—have had a share of the prize if she had lived. If she had received the accolade, one of the other scientists, presumably Wilkins, would have had to be left out, because a single Nobel Prize is never divided among more than three people. (Anne Sayre, however, suggested that a possible alternative would have been to give Watson and Crick the prize in physiology or medicine and assign the same year's prize in chemistry to Wilkins and Franklin.)

J. D. Bernal and, later, Anne Sayre thought that the decision makers in Sweden "could hardly have . . . overlooked" Franklin, as Sayre wrote, if she had been alive. On the other hand, the 1962 prize was given, not just for the discovery of DNA's structure in 1953, but "for . . . discoveries concerning the molecular structure of nucleic acids and its significance for information transfer in living material." On that basis, a good case could be made for giving the prize to Wilkins even if Franklin had been alive. Franklin worked on DNA for only two years, whereas Wilkins's studies of the molecule spanned more than a decade; his work began before she came to King's and continued long after she left. As Wilkins wrote in his autobiography, "King's' share of the Nobel Prize . . . was awarded for a large body of work stretching from the late 1940s to the early 1960s."

This is not to say that Rosalind Franklin might not have become a Nobel laureate if cancer had not so cruelly cut short her career. Aaron Klug, Franklin's last and best collaborator, and the rest of her team continued their research on viruses after Franklin's death, first at Birkbeck and then, beginning in 1962, at the new molecular biology laboratory that Max Perutz established at the Cavendish in Cambridge. In 1982, Klug was awarded the Nobel Prize in chemistry for his work on virus structure. Unlike Watson, Crick, and Wilkins, Klug praised Franklin warmly in his Nobel lecture, saying that she had introduced him to the study of viruses and shown him how to "tackle large and difficult problems." In an interview published on a Web site connected with "Secret of Photo 51," a *Nova* (Public Broadcasting System) television program about Franklin and the discovery of DNA, physicist Lynne Elkin offered the opinion that if Franklin had lived, she might well have sat on the Stockholm stage next to Klug.

## CRUEL CARICATURE

By the late 1960s, Rosalind Franklin had become little more than a painful but fading memory in the minds of her friends and coworkers and an occasional citation in the papers of other scientists. According to Vittorio Luzzati, quoted in "Secret of Photo 51," Franklin's role in determining the structure of DNA might been lost to all but the most detailed scientific histories—except for James Watson.

In 1965, Watson decided to write a short, informal account of the famous discovery. Told in a light and breezy style, with a minimum of technical details, his book aimed to show the public "how science is really done." He wanted it to counteract the view, presented in too many old movies and worshipful biographies, that scientists always act from pure and selfless motives. The result was what Watson biographer Victor K. McElheny terms "the most indiscreet memoir in the history of science."

In his book, which came to be called *The Double Helix,* Watson attempted to re-create as closely as possible the feelings and reactions to people that he had had as an immature young man of 25. Many of those reactions were neither accurate nor kind, especially the ones concerning Rosalind Franklin. His book portrayed "Rosy," as he called her—a nickname she had always despised, though Maurice Wilkins and others at King's College often used it behind her back—as an unattractive, badly dressed woman, lacking the intelligence to interpret her own X-ray data correctly and too possessive to share it with others who might have done a better job. The first paragraphs in the book that refer to her set the tone:

> It was increasingly difficult to take Maurice [Wilkins]'s mind off his assistant, Rosalind Franklin. . . . Maurice, a beginner in X-ray diffraction work,

wanted some professional help and hoped that Rosy, a trained crystallographer, could speed up his research. Rosy, however, did not see the situation this way. She claimed that she had been given DNA for her own problem and would not think of herself as Maurice's assistant. . . .

By choice she did not emphasize her feminine qualities. Though her features were strong, she was not unattractive and might have been quite stunning had she taken even a mild interest in clothes. This she did not. There was never lipstick to contrast with her straight black hair, while at the age of thirty-one her dresses showed all the imagination of English blue-stocking [bookish] adolescents. . . .

Clearly Rosy had to go or be put in her place. The former was obviously preferable because, given her belligerent moods, it would be very difficult for Maurice to maintain a dominant position that would allow him to think unhindered about DNA. . . . The thought could not be avoided that the best home for a feminist was in another person's lab.

At the time of the book's publication and afterward, commentators speculated on why Watson made his portrait of Franklin such a cruel caricature. Part of the reason may have been that Watson had a genuine problem in appreciating women scientists, especially outspoken ones. Rita Levi-Montalcini (1909–   ), who won a share of the Nobel Prize in physiology or medicine in 1986 for her discovery of nerve growth factor, a substance that makes nerve cells grow and mature, met Watson in early 1947, while he was still doing graduate work at the University of Indiana; she wrote in her autobiography, *In Praise of Imperfection*, that "he took no interest in me whatsoever." Watson paid equally little attention to corn geneticist Barbara McClintock (1902–92), a scientist at Cold Spring Harbor Laboratories, whose director Watson became in 1968. Watson once described McClintock to a visiting scientist as "just an old bag who'd been hanging around Cold Spring Harbor for years." The "old bag" became another Nobel laureate—in 1983, when she was 81 years old.

Some of *The Double Helix*'s reviewers thought that Watson's reasons for describing Franklin the way he did were at least partly literary. Although the events in the book actually happened, Maurice Wilkins, for one, described Watson's book (to Brenda Maddox) as more of a "novel" than a work of nonfiction. In order to be interesting, a novel must have conflict: Someone, or something, must oppose the book's main character. In *The Double Helix*, Watson sets up two such forces: Linus Pauling, the competitor against whom he and Crick are supposedly "racing," and Franklin, who hoards her data and frustrates Wilkins so badly that he is driven to become Watson and Crick's secret ally. Jacob Bronowski, a mathematician and later science popularizer known for writing the public television series *The Ascent of Man,* wrote in a review of Watson's book that Watson gave Franklin the role of the evil witch in his "fairy story."

Other commentators brought up a third possible motive: guilt. Watson knew that his and Crick's actions in obtaining and using Franklin's X-ray data had been criticized, and one way to deflect criticism was to make Franklin appear so unreasonable and personally unpleasant that treating her in a somewhat underhanded way would seem justified. As Anne Sayre sarcastically described this approach, "Where you [must deal with] . . . a bright, uppish, contentious female whose hair-do does not appeal, you can scarcely be blamed for taking whatever advantage of her . . . is available."

## A CONTROVERSIAL BOOK

Before Watson's book was published, he sent copies of its manuscript to Crick, Wilkins, Pauling, and several other people whom his narrative had mentioned. Most reacted with anger, not only at the way they themselves were portrayed, but at the treatment Watson meted out to Franklin. Max Perutz, for example, later wrote in the London *Daily Telegraph,* "I was furious about his maligning that gifted girl who could not defend herself." Even the usually mild-mannered Wilkins wrote pointedly to Watson, "Is there any mention in your book that she died?"

To soothe his critics, Watson modified some parts of the book. He did not change what he had written about Franklin, but he added an epilogue that praised her scientific work and referred to both the difficulties she must have faced as a female scientist and her early death. Several of the people mentioned in the book still objected strongly to it, however. According to Brenda Maddox, Wilkins, for instance, wrote to the Harvard University Press, which was planning to publish the book (Watson was a professor at Harvard at the time), that the book was "unfair to me, to Dr. Crick and to almost everyone mentioned except Professor Watson himself." Crick complained that the book invaded his privacy and was "a violation of friendship." Victor McElheny, author of *Watson and DNA,* writes that both Wilkins and Crick "hinted at legal action" if the book appeared.

After reading these angry letters, Harvard president Nathan Pusey and the other members of the Harvard Corporation, the university's governing board, in 1967 ordered the press to cancel the book—an almost unheard-of action. Atheneum Press, a new commercial publishing house, picked it up, however, and published it in February 1968. (Wilkins and Crick did not try to stop the Atheneum publication; McElheny says that they simply did not want the prestigious name of Harvard associated with the book.)

A variety of reviewers, including several eminent scientists, commented on *The Double Helix*. Some, such as Philip Morrison (1915–2005), a professor of physics at the Massachusetts Institute of Technology, writing in the popular magazine *Life*, praised Watson for showing scientists as real people with common human flaws. Others criticized Watson's harsh portraits of some of

## WOMEN IN SCIENCE TODAY: TRYING TO HAVE IT ALL

Women scientists are far more common today than in Rosalind Franklin's time. In a January 20, 2009, article in the *New York Times*, "In 'Geek Chic' and Obama, New Hope for Lifting Women in Science," by Natalie Angier, Joan Burrelli of the National Science Foundation stated that women earned only 8 percent of science and engineering doctorates in the United States in 1959, but in 2006 they accounted for 40 percent. Their strides have been much greater in some fields than others, however. More than a quarter of the country's full professors in life sciences in 2009 are women, but in physics, closely related to Franklin's field of physical chemistry, the figure is only 6 percent.

New laws and greater cultural acceptance of women in science make obvious discrimination less likely today, but women scientists still face some of the same difficulties that Franklin experienced. According to Brenda Maddox, Franklin seemed to doubt that a woman could do justice to both a career and a family, even though some of her woman friends had both. Social science researchers Mary Ann Mason and Marc Goulden of the University of California, Berkeley, found that 70 percent of male tenured professors (those with permanent academic positions) in the United States who answered their survey were married and had children, but this was true of only 44 percent of female tenured professors. "Men can have it all, but women can't," Mason told Natalie Angier in a telephone interview.

the characters, including Franklin. For example, André Lwoff (1902–94), a Nobel Prize–winning physiologist, wrote in the July 1968 *Scientific American* that Watson's portrayal of Franklin was "cruel."

The reading public had no such qualms. Watson's lively, gossipy tone, the suspense of the "race" story, and the thrill of being taken behind the scenes of a great discovery captivated even people who knew or cared little about science. The book became a best seller and has remained so. McElheny reported that as of 2004 the book had sold more than 1 million copies, and it is still in print.

## OTHER VIEWS OF FRANKLIN

Anne Sayre, a close friend of Rosalind Franklin's, was not content to let Watson's portrait of Franklin stand as the public's only perception of her. In 1974, Sayre published a biography of Franklin that she hoped would correct the impression left by Watson's book. She blamed most of Franklin's problems on discrimination and mistreatment that Franklin had received because she was a woman. Later critics have said that Sayre made mistakes of her own; for example, she claimed that there had been only one other woman in the King's College laboratory, but science historian Horace Freeland Judson reported in *The Eighth Day of Creation* that eight of the 31 laboratory members were women.

Sayre's book, which also attracted considerable attention, turned Franklin into what later biographer Brenda Maddox called a "wronged heroine" of feminism. Several people who knew Franklin well have said that this view would have irritated her almost as much as Watson's portrayal. Both Aaron Klug and Jenifer Glynn, Franklin's sister, maintain that Franklin never saw herself as a feminist; she was simply a scientist, and her gender was—or should have been—unimportant. Francis Crick wrote in *What Mad Pursuit* that Klug told him "Rosalind would have hated" Sayre's well-intentioned biography.

Klug himself, who had inherited Franklin's scientific papers and manuscripts, made a more serious attempt to restore her reputation by writing several articles in *Nature* about her role in the determination of DNA's structure. One of these, "Rosalind Franklin and the Double Helix," appeared in 1974, the year in which Sayre's book was published. Klug's article described a newly discovered manuscript dated March 17, 1953—an early draft of the paper that ultimately appeared next to Watson and Crick's in *Nature,* written before Franklin had learned about their discovery. This manuscript showed, Klug wrote, that Franklin at that time was very close to working out the structure of DNA for herself.

In 2003, Brenda Maddox, a British author of several prizewinning biographies, published *Rosalind Franklin: The Dark Lady of DNA,* a biography longer, more extensively researched, and more balanced than Sayre's. This book drew on family letters and scientific notebooks that had not been available to Sayre. Maddox stated that viewing Franklin merely as a symbol of discrimination against women did the scientist's memory as much of a disservice as Watson's harsh and superficial sketch. By focusing primarily on the dramatic events surrounding the DNA discovery, this approach neglected Franklin's substantial scientific achievements before and after that time.

All this controversy and publicity have brought Rosalind Franklin's name and story into the public eye and helped to earn for her memory some of the recognition that she did not survive long enough to receive during her life. In 1995, for example, Newnham College named a new graduate residence after Franklin and put a bust of her in its garden. Birkbeck's School of Crystallography opened a Rosalind Franklin laboratory in 1997, and in 2000, King's College named a new research facility, the Franklin-Wilkins Building, after Franklin and the coworker she disliked so much. The U.S. National Cancer Institute and the British Royal Society established awards for women scientists in Franklin's name in 2001 and 2003 respectively. In 2004, the Finch University of Health Sciences, part of the Chicago Medical School, changed its name to the Rosalind Franklin University of Medicine and Science. Columbia University awarded Franklin a posthumous, honorary Horwitz Prize in 2008 "for her seminal contributions to the discovery of the structure of DNA." The Rosalind Franklin Society, established in Franklin's honor and headquartered in New Rochelle, New York, "recognizes, fosters, and makes known the important contributions of women in science." All these honors no doubt would have pleased Franklin, but she probably would have been happiest to know that her work as a scientist—the aspect of her life that clearly meant the most to her—has been so well remembered.

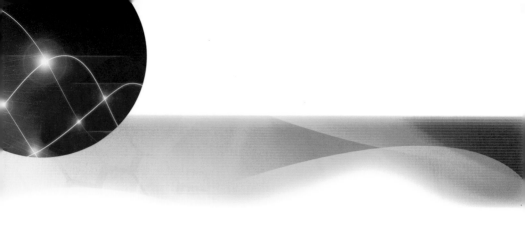

# Conclusion

During her all-too-short career, Rosalind Franklin contributed to three areas of science: the study of forms of carbon, the study of DNA and genes, and the study of viruses. Major advances in all three of these fields have grown out of her work.

## CARBON-FIBER COMPOSITES

Franklin's studies of carbon, especially her classification of carbon materials into those that form graphite on heating and those that do not, led directly to the invention of *carbon-fiber composites*. These materials consist of hard plastic, usually epoxy, in which graphite fibers have been embedded. Carbon-fiber composites are expensive, but they currently have a better strength-to-weight ratio than anything else humans can make. When engineers want a material that is lightweight yet stronger than steel, they turn to carbon-fiber composites.

Carbon-fiber composites can be made in several ways. One of the most common techniques is to place sheets of carbon-fiber cloth in a mold shaped like the product being manufactured, such as part of a car or plane. Epoxy or other liquid plastic is then poured into the mold, and the material is heated or dried in air to harden it. In another technique, a single sheet of carbon fabric is shaped into a thin shell, and the shell is filled with a mixture of plastic resin and fiberglass (glass-reinforced plastic).

Rosalind Franklin's research on forms of carbon led to the invention of carbon-fiber composites, which have greater strength per unit of weight than any other material that humans can make. They are used in advanced technology such as NASA's PIK-20E motor-glider sailplane, shown here during a research flight in 1991. *(NASA Dryden Flight Research Center [NASA-DFRC])*

One use of carbon-fiber composites is to reinforce structures such as bridges and buildings. This material makes the structures much stronger (often twice as strong as before) and more able to resist damage from heavy use or from the shaking produced by earthquakes. Expensive as the composites are, strengthening old structures in this way is often far cheaper than replacing them. Carbon-fiber composites can be used to reinforce concrete, steel, cast iron, masonry (stonework), and wood.

Carbon-fiber composites are also used in a number of consumer products. One of the most popular uses is in racing cars such as Formula One cars, which can travel at speeds greater than 200 miles per hour (320 km/hr). A combination of light weight and tremendous strength is essential in such cars. The composites have usually been considered too expensive to use in ordinary cars, but some high-priced models now include them. Carbon-fiber composites have also become common in spacecraft and in aircraft, ranging from tiny ultralights to large commercial planes such as the Boeing 787 Dreamliner. They are used in some brands of racing bicycles, motorcycles, boats, guitars and other musical instruments, and sports equipment as well.

## GENETIC ENGINEERING

The discovery of the DNA molecule's structure, to which Rosalind Franklin contributed so much, has led not only to an understanding of what genes are and how they work but to the discovery of ways to alter and combine genes for the benefit of humans. This technique, often called *genetic engineering,* is at the root of today's biotechnology industry.

Genetic engineering, in a sense, began in a Hawaiian delicatessen in November 1972. Two scientists, Stanley N. Cohen (1935–   ) of Stanford University and Herbert Boyer (1936–   ) of the University of California, San Francisco, met there by chance while they were attending a conference in Honolulu, Hawaii. They found that they were working in related areas of genetic research. Boyer was studying *restriction enzymes,* proteins that certain bacteria make to cut apart the strands of nucleic acid in invading viruses and thereby render the viruses harmless. (*Enzymes* are a large group of proteins that make chemical reactions occur in cells.) Cohen was doing research on *plasmids,* small, ring-shaped pieces of DNA that carry part of the genetic information in some kinds of bacteria.

The two researchers quickly realized that their experiments might be combined in an interesting way. Boyer's "molecular scissors" enzymes sliced through strands of DNA whenever they found a particular sequence of bases, but they were not very sharp. Instead of cutting cleanly through DNA's dou-

Stanley N. Cohen of Stanford University was one of the two scientists who invented genetic engineering (recombinant DNA) after they met by chance at a Hawaiian delicatessen in late 1972. At the time, Cohen was working with ring-shaped pieces of DNA called plasmids, which carry small numbers of genes in certain bacteria. *(National Library of Medicine)*

Herbert Boyer, the other inventor of genetic engineering, is shown here. Boyer was at the University of California, San Francisco, when he and Stanley Cohen performed the first genetic engineering experiments in 1973. He and venture capitalist Robert Swanson founded Genentech, the first company to be based on recombinant DNA, in 1976. *(Steve Northup/Time-Life Pictures/ Getty Images)*

ble helix, they left an incomplete single strand dangling from each end of each broken piece. The two scientists reasoned that, just as happens when DNA reproduces naturally, the bases in this strand should attract other bases that would complete their usual pairings in the double helix. This meant that the sequence from one snipped piece of DNA should attach easily to the opposite end of another piece of DNA that had been cut by the same enzyme, even if the two DNA fragments came from different kinds of living things. Boyer and Cohen hoped they could break open plasmids from two of the types of bacteria in Cohen's laboratory and then combine them with this technique. Other enzymes called *ligases* could be used to glue the "sticky ends" together.

Boyer and Cohen carried out their first experiment in spring 1973 with plasmids from two different strains, or subspecies, of the intestinal bacterium *Escherichia coli,* which is usually harmless and has been used in innumerable genetic experiments. One plasmid carried a gene that made the bacteria resistant to the antibiotic tetracycline, and the other contained a gene that produced resistance to kanamycin, a different antibiotic. The scientists used Boyer's enzymes to create combined plasmids that included both genes, then put these plasmids into bacteria that would normally be killed by both types of antibiotics. When the altered bacteria were placed in a laboratory dish containing nutrient medium dosed with tetracycline and kanamycin, some of them survived, which proved that both of their newly acquired resistance genes were functioning.

Cohen and Boyer went on to put a gene from a frog into a bacterial plasmid and showed that it too functioned when the plasmid was inserted into living bacteria. Furthermore, the plasmid was copied each time the bacteria reproduced, so the change was permanent and inheritable. In essence, the two researchers had created a new kind of microorganism.

Cohen called his and Boyer's new technique *recombinant DNA*. Other molecular biologists were quick to realize its value. After hearing Boyer describe the work at a scientific meeting in 1973, according to Edwin Shorter's book on the development of the National Institutes of Health, *The Health Century*, one scientist summed up everyone's reaction by saying, "Well, now we can put together any DNA we want to."

In the decades following Boyer and Cohen's discovery, genetic engineering has led to new drugs and techniques for battling disease. It has produced ways to increase the crops that feed the world's growing human population and make them more resistant to weeds and parasites. However, this technique is also highly controversial. Critics claim that genetically modified crops threaten the environment, human health, or both. They fear that microorganisms altered deliberately by terrorists or arising naturally from those modified for other purposes could produce unstoppable plagues that might destroy humanity. The long-term effects of genetic engineering will not be known for many generations to come.

## "BACKWARDS" VIRUSES

Building on the discoveries that Rosalind Franklin, Aaron Klug, and others made about the structure of viruses, researchers have learned how viruses insert their genetic material into cells and reproduce. Most viruses simply force the cell's gene-copying machinery to copy the virus's genes and create new viruses, but some viruses insert their genomes permanently into the cell's own genome. These viruses are called *retroviruses* ("backwards viruses") because they can copy RNA (the nucleic acid in the viruses' genomes) into DNA—something Francis Crick had held in the 1950s to be impossible.

# Recombinant DNA

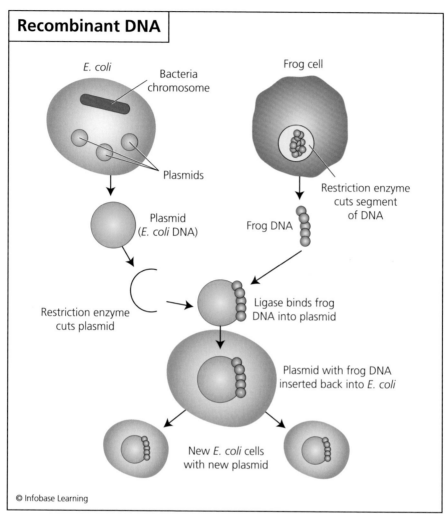

E. coli

Bacteria chromosome

Plasmids

Plasmid (E. coli DNA)

Restriction enzyme cuts plasmid

Frog cell

Restriction enzyme cuts segment of DNA

Frog DNA

Ligase binds frog DNA into plasmid

Plasmid with frog DNA inserted back into E. coli

New E. coli cells with new plasmid

© Infobase Learning

In one genetic engineering experiment, Cohen and Boyer broke up cells of E. coli and took out small ring-shaped pieces of DNA called plasmids. They then used a restriction enzyme to cut the plasmids open. They used the same enzyme to produce segments of DNA from the cells of frogs. The bacterial and frog DNA segments joined together because of the complementary "sticky ends" of single-stranded DNA attached to each segment. The scientists used a ligase, another type of enzyme, to bind the segments together, creating a new plasmid that contained frog and bacterial DNA. The researchers inserted the plasmids carrying the foreign genes into other E. coli bacteria and showed that the foreign genes could make their normal proteins. When the bacteria multiplied, the added genes were duplicated along with the bacteria's own genetic material.

Retroviruses have proved to be involved in several serious diseases that affect humans. Some, for instance, can produce cancer. New York virologist Peyton Rous (1879–1970) suggested as early as 1912 that a type of cancer in chickens was caused by a virus. This virus, now called the Rous sarcoma virus, and several other viruses that cause cancer in animals have proved to be retroviruses. In 1979, Robert Gallo (1937–   ), working at the National Cancer Institute (part of the National Institutes of Health), identified the human T-cell (a type of blood cell in the immune system) leukemia virus, the first virus shown to be able to cause cancer in humans. It, too, is a retrovirus. Most human cancers are not caused by viruses, but several retroviruses can produce it.

The most famous retrovirus of all is the *human immunodeficiency virus (HIV)*, which causes AIDS (acquired immune deficiency syndrome). Luc Montagnier (1932–   ) and his coworkers at the Institut Pasteur in Paris, France, discovered this virus in 1983. The virus attaches itself to certain cells in the immune system and destroys them, thereby rendering the system helpless against invading microorganisms. First brought to medical attention in 1981, AIDS has become a devastating plague in Africa, Asia, and many other parts of the world. The spread of the virus to the United States in the 1980s triggered a nationwide panic that ostracized those who contracted it. Drugs to keep the virus somewhat under control have been developed, but scientists are still searching for a vaccine or cure. Their understanding of this deadly virus's structure, like many other discoveries about viruses, is an indirect descendant of Rosalind Franklin's research—her legacy to the scientific world.

# Chronology

**1869**
Friedrich Miescher discovers nucleic acid

**1898**
Martinus Beijerinck claims that tobacco mosaic disease is caused by an unknown organism smaller than bacteria, which he calls a virus

**1912**
William Henry Bragg and William Lawrence Bragg invent X-ray crystallography

**July 25, 1920**
Rosalind Elsie Franklin is born in London

**1938**
On the basis of his X-ray photographs, William Astbury speculates that the DNA molecule is shaped like a helix

**October 1938**
Franklin begins studies at Newnham College, part of Cambridge University

**September 3, 1939**
Britain declares war on Germany

**July 1940**
German bombing of Britain begins

**1941**
Franklin earns "titular" bachelor's degree in physical chemistry from Cambridge; J. D. Bernal and Isidore Fankuchen take the first X-ray photographs of tobacco mosaic virus

**1942–1945**
Franklin studies the microscopic structure of coal, including changes produced by heat and pressure, as part of the Coal Utilisation Research Association (CURA), a British government agency

**1944**
Oswald Avery publishes paper offering evidence that DNA is the carrier of genetic information; Erwin Schrödinger publishes *What Is Life?*

**May 1945**
World War II ends in Europe with Germany's defeat

**June 1945**
Franklin earns Ph.D. from Cambridge for her coal research

**1946**
Franklin's first scientific papers are published; her wartime service with CURA ends

**1947–1950**
Franklin continues research on forms of carbon and learns X-ray crystallography at a French government chemistry laboratory in Paris; determines that forms of carbon can be divided into two groups

**spring 1950**
Franklin meets John Turton Randall and tours his laboratory at King's College, part of the University of London

**May 1950**
Rudolf Signer gives a sample of purified DNA gel to Maurice Wilkins of King's College

**June 1950**
Franklin obtains a Turner-Newall fellowship to do research in Randall's laboratory

**late 1950**
Wilkins and Raymond Gosling take X-ray photographs of Signer's DNA

**December 1950**
In a letter, Randall tells Franklin that she and Gosling will be working independently on DNA

**January 5, 1951**
Franklin begins research at King's College

**April 1951**
Linus Pauling and Robert Corey show that many protein molecules have a helix shape

**May and July 1951**
Wilkins gives lectures about X-ray photography of DNA that impress James Watson and Francis Crick

**September 1951**
Franklin and Gosling discover that DNA exists in a "dry" (A) form and a "wet" (B) form

**October 1951**
Randall orders Franklin to concentrate on the A form of DNA, leaving the B form to Wilkins; Watson joins Cavendish Laboratory at Cambridge and meets Crick

**November 21, 1951**
Franklin gives a talk on her DNA X-ray work at King's College, which Watson attends

**late November 1951**
Watson and Crick complete a model of the DNA molecule; Franklin tells them it is incorrect

**December 1951**
Lawrence Bragg orders Watson and Crick to stop working on DNA; Franklin looks for a research position outside King's College

**January 1952**
Franklin and Gosling begin applying Patterson functions to their photos of the A form of DNA

**May 1952**
Franklin takes excellent photo of the B form of DNA (Photo 51), then sets it aside

**June 1952**
Franklin arranges to transfer to Birkbeck College at the beginning of 1953

**July 18, 1952**
Franklin and Gosling conclude that the A form of DNA cannot be a helix

**mid-December 1952**
Peter Pauling tells Watson and Crick that his father, Linus Pauling, has worked out a structure for DNA

**January 26, 1953**
Gosling gives Franklin's Photo 51 to Wilkins

**January 28, 1953**
Watson and Crick see a draft of Linus Pauling's paper and detect a major mistake in it; Franklin gives her last seminar at King's College

**January 30, 1953**
Watson visits King's and argues with Franklin; Wilkins shows him Franklin's Photo 51; Watson sees it as proof that the DNA molecule is a helix

**February 4, 1953**
Watson and Crick begin building a new model of the DNA molecule

**February 12, 1953**
Max Perutz shows Watson and Crick a report containing valuable unpublished data from Franklin; Crick concludes on the basis of this information that the DNA molecule must contain two chains with sequences of bases that run in opposite directions

**February 24, 1953**
Franklin concludes that both the A and the B forms of DNA have helix shapes

**February 28, 1953**
Watson realizes that an adenine base on one chain of the DNA molecule always pairs with a thymine base on the other chain; similarly, guanine always pairs with cytosine

**March 1, 1953**
Franklin transfers to J. D. Bernal's laboratory at Birkbeck College (University of London)

**March 7, 1953**
Watson and Crick complete their DNA model

**March 12, 1953**
Wilkins sees Watson and Crick's model and believes that it is correct

**March 17, 1953**
Franklin writes a draft of a paper showing that she has almost solved the DNA molecule's structure independently of Watson and Crick

**March 1953**
Crick proposes that genetic information is encoded in the sequence of bases in the DNA molecule

**early April 1953**
Linus Pauling sees Watson and Crick's model and is impressed

**April 25, 1953**
Watson and Crick's paper announcing the structure of DNA, accompanied by papers from Franklin and Wilkins, appears in *Nature*

**May 30, 1953**
Watson and Crick publish a second paper in *Nature,* explaining how their proposed structure could allow DNA to encode genetic information and reproduce itself

**late 1953**
Franklin begins taking X-ray photos of tobacco mosaic virus; George Gamow proposes that sets of three bases could be the "code words" in nucleic acids; Watson returns to the United States

**early 1954**
Franklin applies Patterson calculations to her virus photographs; is invited to speak on coal at Gordon Research Conference in the United States

**August–October 1954**
Franklin visits the United States for the first time, speaks at the Gordon conference, and visit several virology laboratories

**late 1954**
Franklin meets Aaron Klug, and he joins her in her research

**1955**
Franklin adds new members to her research team; claims that all TMV particles, and all of the virus's protein subunits, have the same size and that the subunits are arranged in a helix

**1956**
Franklin and Don Caspar show that the RNA in TMV coils among the virus's protein subunits rather than lying in the virus's central core; Franklin travels to the United States again, speaks at the Gordon conference on nucleic acids, and revisits virology laboratories; Lawrence Bragg asks Franklin to make models of viruses for the upcoming World's Fair in Belgium

**late 1956**
Franklin is diagnosed with ovarian cancer and has surgery to remove her ovaries and the tumors

**early 1957**
Franklin's team investigates similarities between spherical plant viruses and ribosomes

**July 1957**
U.S. National Institutes of Health awards Franklin's group a grant to cover three years of work; Franklin begins research on poliovirus

**November–December 1957**
Franklin is treated for advanced cancer

**February 1958**
Birkbeck awards Franklin the academic title of research associate in biophysics

**April 16, 1958**
Franklin dies of cancer

**1958**
Matthew Meselson and Franklin Stahl prove that Watson and Crick's theory about the way DNA reproduces itself is correct

**late 1950s**
Wilkins and others assemble further X-ray data that support Watson and Crick's proposed structure for the DNA molecule; Watson studies the structure of RNA and RNA-containing viruses; Crick and Sydney Brenner study the DNA code and how the cell uses it (with the help of RNA) to make proteins

**1960s**
Marshall Nirenberg and others determine the meaning of each "word" of the genetic code

**1962**
Watson, Crick, and Wilkins share the Nobel Prize in physiology or medicine for their work on DNA; Franklin's virus research unit moves to the Cavendish Laboratory

**1965**
Watson writes *The Double Helix*

**1967**
Because of objections to Watson's memoir, Harvard University cancels plans to publish the book

**February 1968**
Atheneum Press publishes *The Double Helix*

**November 1972**
A chance meeting between scientists Stanley N. Cohen and Herbert Boyer sets the stage for the invention of genetic engineering

**spring 1973**
Boyer and Cohen combine genes from two different types of living things for the first time and show that the transferred genes are functional and inheritable

**1974**
Anne Sayre publishes a feminist biography of Franklin; Aaron Klug writes an article in *Nature* offering new evidence that Franklin came close to discovering the structure of DNA

**1979**
Robert Gallo discovers the first virus shown to cause cancer in humans, a retrovirus

**1982**
Aaron Klug wins the Nobel Prize in chemistry for his work on virus structure

**1983**
Luc Montagnier discovers HIV, the retrovirus that causes AIDS

**2000**
King's College opens a new research facility, the Franklin-Wilkins building

**2003**
Brenda Maddox's biography of Franklin appears

**2004**
Finch University of Health Sciences in Chicago changes its name to the Rosalind Franklin University of Medicine and Science

# Glossary

**adenine**   one of four types of bases in DNA and RNA. It always pairs with thymine.

**A form (of DNA)**   one of the two forms of DNA identified by Rosalind Franklin; also called the dry or crystalline form. *See also* **B form.**

**amino acid**   one of 20 kinds of subunits that combine to form proteins.

**angstrom (A)**   a unit of length defined as 0.00000000001 meter, or 0.00000000039 inch; about the size of an atom.

**base**   one of four compounds that attach to the phosphates and sugars in nucleic acids; the sequence of the bases in the nucleic acid molecule carries the genetic code.

**B form (of DNA)**   one of the two forms of DNA identified by Rosalind Franklin; also called the wet form, it appears at high humidity and is the form of DNA found in nature.

**biophysics**   the branch of science that applies the rules of physics to biology.

**carbon-fiber composites**   a group of exceptionally strong, lightweight materials formed from carbon fibers embedded in plastic.

**chromosome**   one of a number of long, spiral bodies in the nucleus of a cell; chromosomes, which are composed of protein and DNA, carry inherited information.

**crystal**   a solid in which the atoms and molecules are arranged in a regular, repeating pattern.

**cytoplasm**   the jellylike substance that fills the main part of a cell.

**cytosine**   one of four types of bases in DNA and RNA. It always pairs with guanine.

**deductive reasoning**   a form of reasoning that proposes a general explanation for a phenomenon, then tests it against specific facts or predictions. *See also* **inductive reasoning.**

**DNA (deoxyribonucleic acid)**   one of two nucleic acids; the carrier of genetic information in most living things. *See also* **RNA.**

**enzyme**    one of a large group of proteins that make chemical reactions occur in cells.

**gene**    a sequence of bases in DNA that contains the code for one type of protein or carries out one task, such as starting or stopping the action of another gene.

**genetic engineering**    the process of deliberately altering genes or combining genes from different species of living things in order to benefit humans.

**genetics**    the branch of science that studies the transmission of inherited information.

**genome**    an organism's complete collection of genetic material.

**graphite**    a form of carbon, used as (among other things) the "lead" in pencils.

**guanine**    one of four types of bases in DNA. It always pairs with cytosine.

**heavy-atom isomorphous replacement**    a technique in which a few atoms of a heavy element such as mercury or lead are substituted for atoms in a virus or other large molecule; comparing the X-ray patterns of the original and altered molecules shows the molecules' structure more clearly than standard X-ray crystallography.

**helix**    a coiled curve, like a spring or a corkscrew.

**hemoglobin**    an iron-containing protein that gives blood its color and carries oxygen throughout the body.

**human immunodeficiency virus (HIV)**    the retrovirus that most scientists agree is the cause of AIDS (acquired immunodeficiency syndrome).

**hypothesis**    an untested idea or theory.

**inductive reasoning**    a form of reasoning that examines large numbers of specific facts in order to work out a general theory or explanation. *See also* **deductive reasoning.**

**ligase**    a type of enzyme that can join together two separated strands of DNA.

**messenger RNA**    a form of RNA that is copied from the DNA in a cell's nucleus; it travels into the cytoplasm, carrying the code for making proteins into the part of the cell where these molecules can be assembled.

**model building**    a technique for creating three-dimensional images of molecules, based on knowledge of their atoms and chemical bonds derived from X-ray crystallography and other sources.

**molecular biology**    the branch of science that investigates biological processes by studying the structure and function of the complex molecules in the bodies of living things.

**nucleic acid** one of two acidic compounds (ribonucleic acid and deoxyribonucleic acid) found in the nucleus and, sometimes, other parts of cells. *See also* **DNA, RNA.**

**nucleotide** a subunit of a nucleic acid molecule, consisting of a phosphate, a sugar, and a base.

**nucleus** the central body of a cell, which contains its genetic information.

**Patterson functions** a type of complex mathematical calculations that can be applied to measurements from X-ray photographs to determine the structure of molecules.

**phosphate** a compound containing the element phosphorus.

**physical chemistry** the branch of science that applies physics to chemistry.

**plasmid** a ring-shaped piece of DNA that carries certain genes in some types of bacteria.

**poliomyelitis (polio)** a human disease, caused by a virus, that can cause paralysis or death; vaccines now prevent it in most parts of the world.

**protein** one of a large group of substances that do most of the work in living cells.

**purines** a group of chemical compounds containing nitrogen; the purines in nucleic acids are adenine and guanine. *See also* **pyrimidines.**

**pyramidines** a group of chemical compounds containing nitrogen, different from purines; the pyrimidines in DNA are cytosine and thymine, but RNA uses the pyramidine uracil in place of thymine. *See also* **purines.**

**quantum mechanics (quantum physics)** the branch of science that studies the behavior of atoms and the particles of which atoms are made.

**recombinant DNA** the technology of combining DNA from two or more different kinds of living things; early name for genetic engineering.

**restriction enzymes** enzymes that slice through the strands of DNA whenever they encounter a certain sequence of bases; certain bacteria make these enzymes to break up the nucleic acid of invading viruses.

**retrovirus** a virus that can copy its RNA genome into the DNA genome of the cells it invades.

**ribosome** a small, round organ in the cytoplasm of cells that helps to assemble proteins from an RNA template.

**RNA (ribonucleic acid)** one of two nucleic acids. Some viruses carry their genes in the form of RNA, but in most living things, RNA's main function is to use the genetic information in DNA to create protein molecules. *See also* **DNA.**

**thymine**    one of four types of bases in DNA. It always pairs with adenine.

**tobacco mosaic virus**    a rod-shaped virus that causes a disease in tobacco plants.

**trait**    a feature or characteristic that can be passed genetically from generation to generation.

**transfer RNA**    a short RNA molecule that carries the code for a single amino acid; it transports that amino acid to messenger RNA during the process of protein formation.

**uracil**    a type of base in RNA that takes the place of thymine in DNA.

**virology**    the branch of science that studies viruses.

**virus**    an extremely small microorganism that can reproduce only inside living cells; it consists of a nucleic acid inside a protein coat.

**X-ray crystallography**    the technique of using X-rays to photograph solids with more or less regular structure and then analyzing the photographs to determine the structure of the molecules in the solids.

# Further Resources

## Books

Crick, Francis. *What Mad Pursuit: A Personal View of Scientific Discovery.* New York: Basic Books, 1988.

*Crick's autobiography, including his description of the discovery of DNA's structure and comments on Rosalind Franklin.*

Glynn, Jenifer. "Rosalind Franklin, 1920–1958." In Edward Shils and Carmen Blacker, eds. *Cambridge Women: Twelve Portraits.* Cambridge: Cambridge University Press, 1996, pp. 267–282.

*Memoir of Franklin written by her younger sister.*

Judson, Horace Freeland. *The Eighth Day of Creation: The Makers of the Revolution in Biology.* New York: Simon and Schuster, 1979.

*Extensive description of DNA structure's discovery and the research that followed it, including long interviews with many of the participants in these events.*

Klug, Aaron. "The Discovery of the DNA Double Helix." In Torsten Krude, ed. *DNA: Changing Science and Society.* New York: Cambridge University Press, 2004, pp. 5–43.

*Article by Franklin's chief collaborator in her post–DNA research emphasizes how close she came to working out the DNA molecule's structure on her own.*

———. "From Macromolecules to Biological Assemblies." In Bo G. Malmström, ed. *Nobel Lectures, Chemistry 1981–1990.* Singapore: World Scientific Publishing Company, 1992. Also available online. URL: http://nobelprize. org/nobel_prizes/chemistry/laureates/1982/klug-lecture.html. Accessed November 15, 2010.

*Klug's Nobel Prize lecture, given on December 8, 1982, describes his work on the structure of viruses and gives credit to Franklin, who introduced him to virus study.*

Maddox, Brenda. *Rosalind Franklin: The Dark Lady of DNA*. New York: HarperCollins, 2002.

*The most detailed and balanced biography of Franklin to date draws on family papers and other sources not available to previous biographers. It covers all her achievements as a scientist, not just her role in the discovery of DNA's structure.*

McElheny, Victor K. *Watson and DNA: Making a Scientific Revolution*. New York: Basic Books, 2004.

*Biography of Watson includes descriptions of his role in the DNA discovery and reactions to his memoir,* The Double Helix.

McGrayne, Sharon Bertsch. *Nobel Prize Women in Science*. Secaucus, N. J.: Birch Lane Press, 1996.

*Book for young adults includes detailed chapter on Franklin, with many quotes from interviews.*

Olby, Robert. *The Path to the Double Helix: The Discovery of DNA*. Seattle: University of Washington Press, 1974.

*Detailed, rather technical description of the research that led up to the working out of the DNA molecule's structure and the discovery of the structure itself.*

Sayre, Anne. *Rosalind Franklin and DNA*. New York: W. W. Norton, 1975.

*This early biography of Franklin by a personal friend stresses the discrimination that Sayre believes Franklin suffered as a woman scientist.*

Schrödinger, Erwin. *What Is Life? The Physical Aspect of the Living Cell*. New York: Macmillan, 1945.

*This book, which recommended approaching biological processes (including the transfer of inherited information) from the standpoint of physics and chemistry, had profound effects on several participants in the search for the molecular structure of DNA.*

Watson, James. *The Double Helix: A Personal Account of the Discovery of the Structure of DNA*. Norton Critical Edition, edited by Gunther S. Stent. New York: W. W. Norton, 1980.

*This edition includes not only the full text of Watson's controversial memoir but an introduction placing the DNA discovery and the book in their historical scientific context, a selection of the most influential reviews of* The Double Helix *(with commentaries by the editor), and six of the original papers about DNA's structure.*

Wilkins, Maurice. *The Third Man of the Double Helix.* New York: Oxford University Press, 2003.

*Wilkins's autobiography supplies the perspective of a scientist whose role in the DNA discovery is often neglected, including his opinions of Rosalind Franklin.*

Yount, Lisa. *Modern Genetics: Engineering Life.* New York: Chelsea House, 2006.

*This book for young adults contains chapters on the discovery of DNA's structure and research that grew out of it, including the development of genetic engineering.*

## Internet Resources

"Double Helix: 50 Years of DNA." In *Nature* (2003). Available online. URL: http://www.nature.com/nature/dna50. Accessed May 14, 2011.

*Web site includes original papers, historical articles, information on the participants in the DNA discovery, animation, and more.*

Franklin, Stephen. "My Aunt, the DNA Pioneer." British Broadcasting Company (April 24, 2003). Available online. URL: http://news.bbc.co.uk/2/hi/science/nature/2895681.stm. Accessed May 14, 2011.

*Brief memoir of Franklin by one of her nephews.*

"Linus Pauling and the Race for DNA." Special Collections, the Valley Library, Oregon State University. Revised February 2009. Available online. URL: http://osulibrary.orst.edu/specialcollections/coll/pauling/dna/index.html. Accessed May 14, 2011.

*Web site focuses on Pauling but also provides a general narrative of the DNA discovery, considerable primary source material, and short biographies of the participants in the discovery, including Rosalind Franklin.*

"The Rosalind Franklin Papers." National Library of Medicine Profiles in Science. Available online. URL: http://profiles.nlm.nih.gov/KR. Accessed May 14, 2011.

*Site provides a detailed biography of Franklin, as well as images and excerpts from her papers.*

"Rosalind Franklin Society." Rosalind Franklin Society. Available online. URL: http://www.rosalindfranklinsociety.org. Accessed May 14, 2011.

*This organization honors Franklin's memory and achievements by recognizing and fostering women's contributions to the life sciences.*

"Rosalind Franklin University of Medicine and Science." Rosalind Franklin University of Medicine and Science. Available online. URL: http://www.rosalindfranklin.edu/DNN. Accessed May 14, 2011.

*This university, founded in 1912 as the Chicago Hospital-College of Medicine, changed its name in 2004 to the Rosalind Franklin University of Medicine and Science to honor Franklin and her work.*

"Secret of Photo 51." Public Broadcasting System, WGBH (Boston). *Nova* (April 22, 2003). Available online. URL: http://www.pbs.org/wgbh/nova/photo51. Accessed May 14, 2011.

*Web site for this television program, originally broadcast in 2003, includes a transcript of the program and several related articles and slide shows, one of which analyzes Franklin's famous X-ray photograph of the B form of DNA in detail.*

"Your Network. Your Resource. Your Voice." Association for Women in Science. Available online. URL: http://www.awis.org. Accessed May 14, 2011.

*Site includes historical and recent data on women's progress in science, such as the percentage of male vs. female members elected to the National Academy of Science by year.*

## Periodicals

Angier, Natalie. "In 'Geek Chic' and Obama, New Hope for Lifting Women in Science." *New York Times,* January 20, 2009.

*Article reviews the progress of women in science and highlights some difficulties that women still face.*

Astbury, W. T. "X-Ray Study of Thymonucleic Acid." *Nature* 141 (April 23, 1938): 747–748.

*Astbury describes the first X-ray photographs of DNA and proposes that the DNA molecule is shaped like a helix.*

Avery, Oswald T., Colin M. MacLeod, and Maclyn McCarty. "Studies on the Chemical Nature of the Substance Inducing Transformation of Pneumococcal Types." *Journal of Experimental Medicine* 79 (January 1944): 137–158.

*Groundbreaking paper showing that pure DNA could transfer inheritable traits from one type of bacteria to another; Avery's experiments provided strong evidence that the carrier of inherited information is DNA rather than protein.*

Bangham, D. H., and Rosalind E. Franklin. "Thermal Expansion of Coals and Carbonised Coals." *Transactions of the Faraday Society* 48 (1946): 289–295.

*Franklin's first published scientific paper, describing some of the research concerning heat's effects on coal structure that she did during her wartime service with the British Coal Utilisation Research Association.*

Bernal, J. D. "Dr. Rosalind E. Franklin." *Nature* 182 (July 19, 1958): 154.

*Short obituary article on Franklin, written by the head of the laboratory at Birkbeck College in which she studied viruses, praises her scientific work.*

Bronowski, Jacob. "Honest Jim and the Tinker Toy Model." *Nation* 206 (March 18, 1968): 381–382.

*In this review, Bronowski states that James Watson's* The Double Helix *has "a quality of innocence and absurdity that children have when they tell a fairy story," with Rosalind Franklin playing the part of the evil witch.*

Creager, Angela N. H., and Gregory J. Morgan. "After the Double Helix: Rosalind Franklin's Research on Tobacco Mosaic Virus." *Isis* 99 (2008): 239–272.

*Long article focuses on Franklin's virus research, a part of her career that is often neglected.*

Crick, Francis. "The Double Helix: A Personal View." *Nature* 248 (April 29, 1974): 766–769.

*Twenty-one years after the publication of Watson and Crick's first papers describing the structure of DNA, Crick looks back on the papers and other scientists' reactions to them.*

———, and J. D. Watson. "The Complementary Structure of Deoxyribonucleic Acid." *Proceedings of the Royal Society* 223 (1954): 80–96.

*This longer paper by Watson and Crick describes their proposed structure for DNA in detail, citing supporting evidence from Franklin and others. It stresses the complementary nature of the sequences of bases in the two chains of the molecule: The two chains have the same sequence running in opposite directions.*

Elkin, Lynne Osman. "Rosalind Franklin and the Double Helix." *Physics Today* 56 (March 2003): 42–48.

*Elkin's article stresses Franklin's contribution to the discovery of the DNA molecule's structure and rejects James Watson's biased view of her.*

Franklin, Rosalind, and R. G. Gosling. "Evidence for 2-Chain Helix in Crystalline Structure of Sodium Deoxyribonucleate." *Nature* 172 (July 25, 1953): 156–157.

*This paper, the first independent confirmation of Watson and Crick's proposed structure for DNA, offers X-ray evidence for believing that both the A and the B forms of DNA have the structure of a two-chain helix.*

———. "Molecular Configuration in Sodium Thymonucleate." *Nature* 171 (April 25, 1953): 740–741.

*This paper by Franklin and Gosling, which appeared with Watson and Crick's first paper on DNA, describes their X-ray findings for the B form of the molecule and states that these findings are "not inconsistent" with the Watson-Crick model. An early draft of this paper, written before Franklin knew about Watson and Crick's proposed structure, suggests that she almost succeeded in working out the structure independently.*

———, A. Klug, and K. C. Holmes. "Structure of Tobacco Mosaic Virus: Location of the Ribonucleic Acid in the Tobacco Mosaic Particle." *Nature* 177 (May 19, 1956): 928–930.

*One of several articles in which Franklin and her research team presented evidence that the RNA in tobacco mosaic virus is coiled among the virus's protein subunits rather than existing separately in the hollow center of the virus.*

Fuller, Watson. "Who Said 'Helix'?" *Nature* 424 (August 2003): 876–878.

*Describes Franklin's discoveries about DNA and criticizes her for not sharing the results of her research with other scientists working on the problem.*

Holt, Jim. "Photo Finish: Rosalind Franklin and the Great DNA Race." *New Yorker,* October 28, 2002.

*Extensive review of Brenda Maddox's biography of Franklin focuses on Franklin's role in the discovery of the DNA molecule's structure.*

Judson, Horace Freeland. "Annals of Science: The Legend of Rosalind Franklin." *Science Digest* (January 1986): 56–59, 78–83.

*According to Judson, feminist claims that Franklin was cheated of her rightful share of credit for the DNA discovery because she was a woman are mistaken.*

Klug, Aaron. "Rosalind Franklin and the Discovery of the Structure of DNA." *Nature* 219 (August 24, 1968): 808–810, 843–844.

*Klug, Franklin's collaborator in her later career, stresses the importance of Franklin's contribution to the discovery of the structure of the DNA molecule and corrects impressions left by James Watson's memoir,* The Double Helix.

———. "Rosalind Franklin and the Double Helix." *Nature* 248 (April 20, 1974): 787–788.

*Brief article describes a recently discovered draft manuscript showing that Franklin almost succeeded in working out the structure of DNA independently of Watson and Crick.*

Lwoff, André. "Truth, Truth, What Is Truth (About How the Structure of DNA Was Discovered)?" *Scientific American* 219 (July 1968): 133–138.

*Review of Watson's* The Double Helix *in which Lwoff points out that Watson's portraits of many participants in the DNA discovery, including Rosalind Franklin, are cruel, but perhaps the book's most unflattering caricature of all is of Watson himself.*

Maddox, Brenda. "The Double Helix and the 'Wronged Heroine.'" *Nature* 421 (January 23, 2003): 407–408.

*Maddox claims that seeing Rosalind Franklin only as a victim of discrimination against women does her reputation as much of a disservice as James Watson's harsh portrait of her.*

Morrison, Philip. "The Human Factor in a Science First." *Life,* March 1, 1968, p. 8.

*In this brief review of Watson's* The Double Helix, *Morrison, a physics professor at the Massachusetts Institute of Technology and the book editor of* Scientific American, *praises Watson for "kill[ing] the myth that great science must be cold, impersonal or detached."*

Olby, Robert. "Quiet Debut for the Double Helix." *Nature* 421 (January 3, 2003): 402–405.

*Science historian Olby states that most scientists in the 1950s gave Watson and Crick's proposed structure for the DNA molecule a lukewarm reception and failed to recognize it as a groundbreaking scientific advance.*

Pauling, Linus, and Robert B. Corey. "A Proposed Structure for the Nucleic Acids." *Proceedings of the National Academy of Sciences* 39 (February 1953): 84–97.

*This article describes Pauling's incorrect three-chain structure for DNA.*

———, and H. R. Branson. "The Structure of Proteins: Two Hydrogen-Bonded Helical Configurations of the Polypeptide Chain." *Proceedings of the National Academy of Science* 37 (1951): 207 ff.

*This important paper by Pauling gave evidence that protein molecules have a helical shape, which encouraged Watson and Crick to believe that nucleic acid molecules might have a similar structure.*

Perutz, Max F. "How the Secret of Life Itself Was Discovered." *Daily Telegraph,* April 27, 1987.

*Short article in which Perutz criticizes Watson's* The Double Helix *for its harsh portrait of Franklin.*

————. "Letter to *Science*." *Science* 164 (June 27, 1969): 1,537–1,538.

*In this letter, Perutz defends his showing the King's College report to the Medical Research Council, which contained valuable unpublished data from Rosalind Franklin, to Watson and Crick.*

Piper, Anne. "Rosalind Franklin: Light on a Dark Lady." *Trends in Biochemical Sciences* 23 (1998): 151–154.

*Biographical sketch of Franklin written by a longtime friend.*

Song, Sora, and Andrea Dorfman. "The Chain of Events." *Time* 161 (February 17, 2003): 53 ff.

*Chronology of major advances in research on DNA from 1951 to 2003.*

Squires, G. L. "The Discovery of the Structure of DNA." *Contemporary Physics* 44 (July–August 2003): 289–305.

*Technical article provides background on the chief discoverers of DNA's structure, including Franklin and details of the X-ray crystallography calculations that revealed the structure.*

Watson, J. D., and F. H. C. Crick. "Genetical Implications of the Structure of Deoxyribonucleic Acid." *Nature* 171 (May 30, 1953): 964–967.

*Watson and Crick's second and longer paper in* Nature, *explaining how their proposed structure for DNA allows the molecule to reproduce itself.*

————. "A Structure for Deoxyribose Nucleic Acid." *Nature* 171 (April 25, 1953): 737–738.

*Watson and Crick's groundbreaking short paper describing their proposed structure for the DNA molecule.*

Wilkins, M. H. F., A. R. Stokes, and H. R. Wilson. "Molecular Structure of Deoxypentose Nucleic Acids." *Nature* 171 (April 25, 1953): 738–740.

*Paper by Wilkins and others at King's College that appeared with Watson and Crick's original paper on DNA, describing X-ray work on DNA from the cells of several types of living things.*

Woods, Gordon. "Rosalind Franklin: Physical Chemist, X-ray Crystallographer and DNA Pioneer." *Chemistry Review* 16 (February 2007): 17–19.

*Brief review of Franklin's career and contributions to the understanding of DNA.*

# Index